"In *ReCreatable*, Kevin has brough[...] [...]hat is contagious and filled with the [...] y a resource that will bring healing and [...] [...]ity. Honest! Hopeful! Thoughtful!"

—**Dr. Jo Anne Lyon**, general superintendent of The Wesleyan Church and founder of World Hope International

"Our creator God has given us this world so that we might live well, but like the earth itself, we are broken. Yet God offers each of us hope—hope for a new earth, and hope for restored hearts. *ReCreatable* extends the blessings of reconciliation to all of us. May we learn to rest in God's healing and enter into His shalom."

—**Matthew Sleeth**, MD, executive director of Blessed Earth and author of *24/6: A Prescription for a Healthier, Happier Life*

"Here is a biblical vision for discipleship and holiness that will resonate with a new generation. In *ReCreatable*, Kevin Scott marks out the ancient but oft-forgotten pathway to living well through the power of the Holy Spirit. Read this book with your family, your congregation, or your small group to discover together how to bring hope and healing to the corner of the world where you live."

—**Dr. Stan Toler**, best-selling author, pastor, teacher, and general superintendent emeritus for the Church of the Nazarene

"In a world that is fractured and broken, Kevin has written a book that beautifully articulates how living and sharing the Kingdom Life brings eternal restoration here and now. *ReCreatable* will move people toward a life of transformation!"

—**Jeremy Summers**, coauthor of *Awakening Grace: Spiritual Practices to Transform Your Soul* and adult spiritual formation movement director for The Wesleyan Church

"The good news is that the Good News is for broken people, and *ReCreatable* maps out how the gospel transforms our brokenness in God's sustainable way. In this practical and inspiring book, Kevin Scott helps us see how God fits the pieces back together again."

David Drury, coauthor of *SoulShift: The Measure of a Life Transformed*

"All of us have brokenness in our lives, but *ReCreatable* reminds us that God is all about restoration. If I had to describe this book in one word, it would be *hope*—hope for all of us, hope for any of us."

—**Rev. Kenneth C. Haugk**, PhD, executive director of Stephen Ministries, www.stephenministries.org

"*ReCreatable* is both heavenly and earthy. This book is rich devotionally with solid, practical application, inspiring a deeper faith."

—**Mark O Wilson**, pastor and author of *Filled Up, Poured Out*

"Kevin Scott's book has given me a whole new vocabulary—with words like *ReCreatable* and phrases like "in a pocket of the kingdom." . . . *ReCreatable* is guaranteed to be a great resource for churches, schools, small groups, and individuals."

—**Derek Cooper**, PhD, director of the Doctor of Ministry program at Biblical Seminary and coauthor of *Hazardous: Committed to the Cost of Following Jesus* and *Unfollowers: Dropouts, Detractors, and Doubters of Jesus*

"A fresh new look at discipleship! . . . Scott's approach to holiness is freeing while also holding to strong biblical truth."

—**Jason Taylor**, lead pastor of The Vertical Church, Yuma, Arizona

"Kevin Scott addresses an important question, which is, how do we keep a sustainable faith while living in a broken world? Anyone looking to sharpen their walk with the Lord will find this book helpful."

—**Dr. Alvin Sanders**, associate executive director of EFCA National Ministries and author of *Bridging the Diversity Gap*

RE CREATABLE

How God Heals the Brokenness of Life

KEVIN SCOTT

Kregel
Publications

ISBN 978-0-8254-4211-7

Printed in the United States of America
14 15 16 17 18 / 5 4 3 2 1

To Debbie,
my wife of twenty-plus years—
Your faith, hope, and love shine brightly.
It is in your presence I most often remember that
God loves me and gave himself for me.
May we live well together for
many years to come.

Ask for the ancient paths, where the good way is;
and walk in it, and find rest for your souls.
—Jeremiah 6:16

We live by mercy if we live.
To that we have no fit reply
But working well and giving thanks,
Loving God, loving one another,
To keep Creation's neighborhood.
—Wendell Berry

If you dare to pray for holiness, humility
or other dangerous things,
God may just give them to you.
—N. T. Wright

CONTENTS

ACKNOWLEDGMENTS

Every book is a collaboration, and this page is my opportunity to say thank you to just a few of the people who have contributed in some way to the writing of this book.

To the excellent staff at the Paradise Cafe in Noblesville, Indiana, for providing the perfect environment for writing this book.

To Ken Haugk, David Paap, Bill McKay, Joel Keen, Joel Bretscher, Steve Glynn, and so many other colleagues at Stephen Ministries, for your friendship and for growing and stretching me in so many ways over the years.

To the scholar, the philosopher, and the farmer—N. T. Wright, Dallas Willard, and Wendell Berry—three men whose insights have uniquely impacted my life. Their work underlies and is woven throughout everything in these pages, such that any contribution I may have made is only by standing on the shoulders of these giants, and others like them.

To Dennis Hillman, Steve Barclift, Dawn Anderson, Bob Hartig, Dave Hill, Noelle Pederson, Adam Ferguson, Leah Mastee, and the rest of the team at Kregel Publications for believing in me and the message of *ReCreatable*.

To my friend Lyn Rayn for her excellent design work on the cover of this book.

To our little pocket of the kingdom in Noblesville, Indiana, for being faithful companions who have often encouraged, strengthened, and challenged me.

To Kenny and Anna Panduku, whose friendship consistently leaves this introvert feeling energized. You are greatly loved and appreciated.

To my mom and dad, brothers and sisters-in-law, aunts and uncles, nieces and nephews, and other relatives, whether they be Scotts, Sales, Mounts, Banishes, d'Ablaings, Johnsons, or whatever other surnames may soon find their way in, I truly could not have been blessed with a better, more supportive family. You know it's true. Even though I rejected the bow tie suggestion.

To my children—Courtney, Lauren, Ethan (with Jesus), and Micah—who make life so fun and rewarding, and who sacrificed many hours of "Dad's going to the coffee shop to write." I love nothing more in this life than to see God re-creating your lives before my very eyes.

To my wife, my lifelong love, Debbie. Thank you for your undying confidence, companionship, sacrifice, and love.

And to Jesus, my Lord and Redeemer, for all of the above and everything else—past, present, and future—thank you. Amen.

INTRODUCTION

On January 19, 2013, Stanley Frank "The Man" Musial passed away. Musial was one of the best, most underrated baseball players ever. But rarely will you hear someone talk about Musial's baseball prowess without quickly adding, "and he was an even better man."

Few modern men have been so deeply rooted in a place. When you think of Stan Musial, you think of St. Louis. And when you think of St. Louis, it won't be long until you think of Stan the Man.

Around St. Louis, where I lived for more than thirty-five years, Stan Musial was known for his approachability, decency, and enjoyment of life. He was also known for his faith, his eternal optimism, and his love for Lil, his wife of *seventy-one* years.

Oh, and he played a mean harmonica. This shy, quiet man learned to play the portable instrument as a way to quickly connect with people. Probably thousands of St. Louisans have stories of meeting Musial out somewhere and him whipping out his harmonica to play a quick rendition of "Take Me Out to the Ball Game."

The printed piece handed out at Stan's funeral featured these lines, written in 1904 by Elisabeth-Anne "Bessie" Anderson Stanley:

He has achieved success who has lived well, laughed
    often, and loved much;
Who has enjoyed the respect of intelligent men and the
    love of little children;
Who has filled his niche and accomplished his ask;
Who has left the world better than he found it;
Who has always looked for the best in others and given
    them the best he had;
Whose life was an inspiration;
Whose memory a benediction.

Stan Musial was such a man.

He lived well.

In many ways, *ReCreatable* is a book about living well.

All of us are broken—some of us more than others, due to the circumstances in our lives. But all of us are ReCreatable. God is in the business of putting broken lives and relationships back together again.

People have all kinds of misconceptions about who God is and what he wants from us. The message of this book is that what God wants *from* you is more about what he wants *for* you: he wants you to experience life in all its fullness, life as he designed it to be when he created the concept.

He wants you, wants all of us, to live well.

And the thing is, as we learn to live well, we find that not only is God putting our broken lives back together again, but he also begins to work through us to help other people find healing in their brokenness as well—often without our even realizing the part we're playing!

From another perspective, *ReCreatable* is about Christian discipleship, learning to walk with Christ.

I am well aware that only a small percentage of book readers actually start by reading the introduction. Obviously, you are one of those people. So I want you to know that these next few paragraphs are some of the most important in the book.

ReCreatable is about how you can become a disciple of Christ, but it's also about how you can become a disciple who *makes disciples*— not all by yourself, but within a pocket of the kingdom with Christ at its head.

The book is structured to make it easy for you to not only read, but also remember and pass on its basic message to others. Being a disciple of Jesus is about becoming a person who

> reflects his glory
> by living well
> in a pocket of the kingdom.

That's the five-seconds-or-less description of a disciple who makes disciples. It's highly portable, just like Stan's harmonica.

We can begin to unpack that definition by adding the book's title, subtitle, and chapter titles, so that we come up with a deeper but still forty-five-seconds-or-less description:

"Reflecting his glory" means that God is taking the **shards** of the world and our broken lives and restoring his **glory** to them. We become a place of **intersection** where people can meet God as he makes us **holy**.

"Living well" means that Christ develops in our hearts a **sustainable** pattern of **faith**, **hope**, and **love**. This is the essence of healing, holiness, and God's glory in us.

"In a pocket of the kingdom" means that the holy life—the attractive life—is lived with other Christians who come together around **Scripture**, **worship**, and **community**, and who welcome others into the kingdom pocket through Christian **mission**.

It is through this process—this story recapitulated in every disciple's life—that **God heals the brokenness of life**. We may be broken, but we are **ReCreatable**.

For those who are ready to go deeper than this forty-five-second definition, you can unpack each of the words bolded above by working your way through the book, chapter by chapter.

Then when you're done, you can pack it all away again in that five-second definition—ready to be pulled out at a moment's notice to share again with each broken person you encounter, as the Holy Spirit leads you.

I hope you will do this. Memorize the five-second and even the forty-five-second description of a disciple. Study the book with your family, with your small group, within your congregation, or in your neighborhood or community. I've provided a group discussion guide with thought-provoking questions that you can use to guide groups through this study, just as I have in my congregation.

What I've tried to give you is a portable message.

If I could, I'd make it possible for you to play it on a harmonica.

Before we jump in, let me offer one quick caveat. This book is about finding healing for life's brokenness, and that is precisely what Christ offers. But it's important to mention that you don't find Christ's healing in a book. You find his healing most often in relationship with a person or people who listen and provide careful attention and support—the kind of caring presence that can and should be found in "pockets of the kingdom."

At times, though, you may need to find a deeper level of care than a group can provide. You may need to seek out the care of a specially trained layperson, such as a Stephen Minister, who can provide one-to-one care during a particularly difficult time.

Some types and levels of brokenness are more complex than a small group or a trained layperson can adequately care for. Certain traumatic or deeply rooted forms of brokenness require the care of a mental health professional.

In any case, while this book describes "how God heals the brokenness of life," his healing touch most often involves relationships with people who are actively caring for you. This book is not a substitute for that.

I write not as a guru but as a fellow companion on the journey. I have many of the same questions, challenges, struggles, and failings as you. Maybe more. I too am a broken person. But by God's grace and mercy, he is putting both you and me back together again.

You are immensely valuable to God. Though you may be aware of brokenness in your life or the lives of those you love, you can be sure that God is capable of picking up the pieces to make beautiful things out of the shards—and more than willing to do so.

Live well!

—Kevin Scott
October 2, 2013
Noblesville, Indiana

Part One

REFLECT HIS GLORY

I am a creature, it is true, but I have a calling
to be the creature glorified.
I must be the creature, but I do not have to be
the creature like the clod in the field,
the cabbage which is rotting in the field as the snow melts.
I am called to be a creature by choice, on the basis of Christ's
finished work, by faith:
the creature glorified.
—Francis Schaeffer

Chapter 1

SHARDS

With his shameful, chaotic, horrible death he has gone to the
very bottom, to the darkest and deepest place of the ruin, and
has planted there the sign that says "Rescued."
—N. T. Wright

Her voice hinted at a barely-controlled panic.

"Umm . . . Mom! Dad!"

The logs in our back porch fire pit were crackling, and we were just beginning to smell the rich, warm scent of fudge brownies through the screen door.

"Mom. Dad. Could you come here? Quick!"

As we made our way into the kitchen, she called us to the oven, where we could see that a minor catastrophe had taken place. Only minutes before, Courtney had placed in the oven a baking pan filled with brownie batter. But in a moment of inexplicable weakness, the glass pan had popped, shattered, and then crumbled.

Deliciously fragrant brownie batter dripped and coated the bottom of the oven. But now it contained an unexpected, unwanted ingredi-ent. Hundreds of tiny glass shards were baking into the batter on the hot surface of the oven floor.

Only moments before, the batter had held such promise. It had smelled so inviting . . . and actually, it still did. But now it was worse than useless—dangerous to touch, perhaps deadly to taste. The glass pan had but one purpose, and it had failed miserably at that task. There was nothing to be done but carefully clean up the mess and throw it away.

Like that glass pan, you also were created for a single, specific pur-pose. And here it is:

> *You were created to reflect God's glory.*

You carry God's image. You're his glory-bearer. And you're called to bear his image and reflect his glory in the midst of the people with whom you live and work. Today.*

It's not your job alone. In fact, it works best when you're among a group of people who are committed to reflecting God's glory together until the earth is "filled with the knowledge of the glory of the Lord as the waters cover the sea" (Hab. 2:14).

But as you might suspect, there's a problem. The mirror of your life is cracked. The reflecting pool has become polluted. God's image in you is now distorted. Like the shattered brownie pan, you begin your journey with God as a broken person, tragically unable to fulfill your specific purpose and calling. You fall short of his glory (Rom. 3:23).

We all do.

---

*See, for example, Genesis 1:26–27; Isaiah 43:7; Matthew 5:16; Romans 8:16–17; Ephesians 1:12; Philippians 2:11; and 1 Corinthians 10:31.

When others look at our lives and relationships, they generally don't see God's glory; instead they see our brokenness. Even as I say that, I feel compelled to assure you that "it's OK." But really, it's far from OK. What I *can* assure you is that it doesn't have to be that way.

Much of our brokenness comes from resisting and rebelling against God's call to become a fully mature human being. But a lot of it is because those around us—parents, spouses, children, friends, neighbors—are broken too. No matter where our brokenness comes from, it's still our brokenness.

Since we're all broken people, we often end up hurting those around us, even those we love—sometimes *especially* those we love. Like those shards of glass baked into a seemingly delicious brownie, we have the potential to injure others and destroy relationships.

It's painful to admit this is true, right? We all want to minimize and normalize our sin even as we magnify the sins of others. After all, it's always easier to see the effects of others' offenses than our own.

Most of us have patterns of sin so deeply engrained in us that we easily convince ourselves that it's just *the way we are.*

Maybe. But it's not who you were created to be.

You were created to be holy, the perfect image of God in all his glory.

When our brownie pan exploded, there was nothing to be done about it. We couldn't put it back together again. It would never again fulfill the purpose for which it was created. We carefully scraped and swept it up and tossed it in the trash.

And when it comes to our broken lives and relationships, it seems much the same. As much as we might want to, we don't seem capable of fixing what's broken.

All of this sounds like very bad news. And, well, it is bad news. But there is good news too. And it can be summed up in five powerful words:

Jesus is Lord and Redeemer.

That is the gospel. That's our promise that God puts broken people back together again.

Long ago, even before God created the world, he mapped out a plan for its redemption and ours. God chose *not* to sweep up the mess—in the world or in your life—and toss it in the trash. Instead he looks at your life (and mine), in whatever state of mess and disarray it may be, and says, "I created it, and I can put it back together again."

You are ReCreatable. Jesus wants to pick up all the broken pieces of your life and fit them back together so you can once again take up your calling to reflect his glory in the place where you do life. You can become a fully mature human being who lives life to the fullest, bringing God glory in the process.

But the first step is to stop denying that you're a mess. It's to own your brokenness.

This might be a tough thing. Some people struggle to see the ways they are broken and how they pass that brokenness on to those around them. Others find it harder to believe that God can redeem anything out of their mess. Whichever tendency you may have, it's time to embrace your identity as a broken person in whom God is restoring the capacity to reflect his glory. Wrestle with this chapter. Own it in your life. You will take a gigantic first step toward living well, reflecting God's glory with your whole life.

Maybe you're not quite ready to recognize and deal with your brokenness. That's OK. Just skip this chapter, go on to the next, and come back later when you feel ready.

But for those of you, the brave ones, who are ready to face your brokenness, let's begin with a look at where it all began.

Three Attitudes That Can Break Relationships

When God lovingly crafted the original man and woman, the bearers of his image, he placed them in a beautiful garden. It was a place that offered the hope of unending joy and harmonious, healthy, satisfying relationships. He gave the man and woman a choice: to reflect his glory with their whole lives or to reject the calling and seek their own pathway.

The choice was summed up in a command that they should avoid eating the fruit from a single, desirable tree in the middle of the garden—the tree of the knowledge of good and evil. God said if they ate the fruit of the tree, they would die (Gen. 2:16–17).

Unfortunately, Adam and Eve were ensnared and enslaved by three seemingly innocuous attitudes.

Discontent

We don't know how long it took—it could have been hours or decades later—but one day, a malevolent spiritual force, manifested somehow in a serpent, tempted Eve to eat the fruit (Gen. 3:1–7). Part of the attraction was simply to do something for herself. The fruit looked delicious and desirable; there seemed no good reason to deny herself the pleasure. Though God had given Adam and Eve all they could ever need or want, Eve found herself desiring what she could not have. Maybe you've been there too. This was the first small step toward brokenness.

Distrust

The serpent continued to seduce Eve, planting seeds of doubt that God had her best interests at heart. In mocking amazement, he asked: "You can't eat from any of the trees? Seriously?" (Gen. 3:1; author's rough paraphrase).

Well, no, God had not said that, and to her credit, Eve corrected the serpent. She said God allowed them to eat from every tree but one. Only the tree in the middle of the garden was forbidden. But then Eve went further: "God won't even let us touch the fruit or we'll die." It was a revealing exaggeration. Eve was leaning in toward a seemingly sympathetic ear.

Sensing the slightest opening, the serpent unleashed the assault. He didn't deny God's existence or that he was the Creator. He didn't even deny that God could tell Adam and Eve what to do. All of that would have been too obvious. Instead, he did something much more devilish.

The serpent denied God could be trusted. Eating the fruit, he said, wouldn't kill them; it would make them stronger and wiser. They would become like God. God didn't want that to happen, he said, and that's why God had forbidden them to eat the fruit (Gen. 3:4–5).

Eve bit. And her growing distrust was a second giant step toward brokenness.

Disregard

Eve's unholy act was surely also a naive one. She could not have understood its implications or its consequences. After all, such a thing had never been done. Eve was not an evil, diabolical person; she had never questioned God or been resentful of him. Not that we know of. She simply made a poor decision in the heat of the moment. We can sympathize with her.

However, what seemed like an insignificant act—reaching out to pick and eat an attractive piece of fruit—was the first, inexcusable act of human rebellion.

Eve knew her Creator and his command. She knew what consequences he had promised. She was fully aware of her disobedience.

By eating the fruit anyway, Eve acted with total disregard for God.

Then she offered the fruit to her husband, and apparently without hesitation, he ate it too.

Three seemingly innocuous attitudes—discontent, distrust, and disregard—proved both dangerous and destructive, and soon the damage was done. Ever since, the heavens and earth, which were created to demonstrate God's glory, have been filled instead with an unending pattern of broken relationships and broken lives.

Museum of Broken Relationships

Innocence is a gift that should never be taken for granted. At first, eating the fruit must have seemed like an insignificant, inconsequential act. But slowly it began to dawn on Adam and Eve that everything had somehow changed, that life would never be the same again. They may have thought they were enjoying a private, personal rebellion; but the effects of their sin were anything but contained. Maybe you can relate. The consequences were immediate, and the devastating reverberations continue today.

By rejecting God's command and eating the fruit, they showed they were capable of something God never intended: unholiness. The thing they didn't know—couldn't know—was that unholiness always leads to brokenness.

God's law is never arbitrary; it is rooted in who he is and in who he created us to be. So sin is not the breaking of an arbitrary rule or law. It is any activity or behavior that is unworthy of a human being—one created in God's image. To sin is not to be human; it is to *degrade* our humanity. Sin makes us less human, not more. That's the tragedy. We fail to be what God—in his infinite wisdom—created us to be: a bearer of God's glory.*

---

*See N. T. Wright, *Romans*, New Interpreter's Bible Commentary (NIBC) (Nashville, TN: Abingdon, 2002), 434.

Through one unholy act, Adam and Eve introduced the reality of unrighteousness and brokenness into every aspect of their lives and relationships—and to all their descendants.

In the town of Zagreb, Croatia, there is a quirky exposition called the Museum of Broken Relationships. Artists Olinka Vistina and Drazen Grubisic created the museum to give a permanent home to some of their cherished mementos from when they were still a couple. As word of the "breakup" museum spread, many other items were donated—sentimental love letters, teddy bears, an axe that was used to destroy furniture after a breakup, and even a prosthetic leg.*

While most of us haven't immortalized our tokens of affection (or spite) in such a public way, we all know the damage and grief that broken relationships leave in their wake. Every relationship and every *kind* of relationship is impacted by human sin and brokenness.

Broken Identity

Sin immediately changed the way Adam and Eve thought of themselves, altering their self-awareness and hacking into their identity. First they noticed they were unclothed. They felt exposed, vulnerable. They couldn't seem to escape one another's gaze. Surely there could be no defense for their unholy act, no one to blame but themselves. For the first time, they experienced guilt and shame. Then, there was fear, and with a most unexpected trigger: the God who had lovingly crafted them (Gen. 3:10).

In one regrettable moment—like that moment when you release the locked car door with your keys still in the ignition—everything was changed. A moment before, Adam and Eve had known only

---

*"Museum of Broken Relationships," Atlas Obscura, accessed April 17, 2013, http://atlasobscura.com/place/museum-odd-broken-relationships.

innocence, satisfaction, confidence, security. Now they were owners of a broken identity. And there was nothing to be done about it.

Brokenness has been part of our identity ever since. Each of us is a unique bundle of insecurities and neuroses. We brew our personal concoction, with varying amounts of guilt, doubt, shame, anxiety, and fear. You may have been dealt a tougher hand than others. Or perhaps you've been fortunate. Either way, you can be sure that your brokenness extends to the way you view yourself.

Broken Trust

With that first unholy act, the man and woman became partners in crime. They even hid out together. But now something was uncomfortable about their relationship; there had been a breach of trust. Before their crime, they were naked and unashamed. Now neither could long endure the gaze of the other. So they sewed some fig leaves together and covered the parts of their bodies they suddenly knew could be exploited. Later, when God questioned them, neither would own their actions. The man blamed his wife and the woman blamed the serpent.

Now it seems we are almost "wired" to distrust one another. We do it without thinking. Our natural instinct—due to our brokenness—is to look out for our own needs and wants first, often to the exclusion and detriment of others. We instinctually serve our own esteem and comfort as we subconsciously try to shore up what was lost in the garden of Eden. If you take an honest look at your relationships, past and present, you'll probably see a pattern of brokenness. And it goes both ways.

Broken Faith

Sin had a devastating effect on Adam's and Eve's relationship with God. After all, he had entrusted his newly created world to them. He was their Creator and Provider; everything they had came from him. After their rebellion, they felt compelled to hide from God. They feared what he would do. Even with their new clothes, they still felt vulnerable and exposed to his gaze. Maybe you've felt that way too.

Adam and Eve were probably unsure how God would respond if he knew they had eaten from the tree. They may have thought for a moment that they could hide the truth from him. Instead of being forthcoming, Adam tried to explain that he hadn't come out to meet God because he was naked.

Unholy acts damage everything they touch, but the damage is most severe in our relationship with the God who created us. Many people today feel they're "alone in the universe." Others feel burdened by the weight of guilt and shame. Yet we are the ones who have broken faith with God by our rebellious behavior. From the moment of the fall, men and women have searched for something, anything, that can fill the void left by this broken relationship, but there is nothing outside of God that can satisfy our need for fellowship with him.

Broken Creation

One final consequence of Adam's and Eve's sin was a broken relationship with God's creation (Gen. 3:14–19). This is the meaning behind the curses God placed on the serpent and on the ground. Ever since, there has always been an element of danger in our interaction with the place where we live. And though the earth provides everything we need for sustenance and life, it does not yield its harvest easily.

Since that day, humanity has had an uneasy relationship with the earth—often appreciating and enjoying it but sometimes also fearing and abusing it. Left to ourselves, we tend to misuse the earth and deplete its natural resources with little thought of preserving or renewing them for future generations.

It is impossible to overstate the immediate and devastating consequences of humanity's fall into sin and rebellion against God. It has led to an unending string of broken relationships with ourselves, others, God, and his creation. Unfortunately, this is what we have come to think of as "being human."

No. "Being human" is to trust God and to reflect his glory in all our relationships. The problem is that sin has diminished and distorted our humanity. That's why God condemned sin itself on the cross (Rom. 8:3).

The pathway to holiness begins with awareness—a deep recognition—of the fact of our brokenness along with a genuine sorrow for the damage we've caused in our relationships. It is painful to take such an inventory, but only then do we truly understand the gift we've been given in God's gracious offer of redemption.

Beyond Brokenness

You may have noticed that in this chapter I've focused on brokenness as the primary result of sin and rebellion. I've only briefly mentioned our guilt before God. This is in no way to diminish its reality. I've focused on brokenness for two reasons. One is that many of us see our brokenness more than our guilt. It's sometimes easier to see how our life is a mess than to comprehend that we must give an account of our actions before a holy God. It's important that we come to terms with our guilt before God; but recognizing the mess we've made is a healthy, attainable first step toward recognizing and accepting our guilt before God.

Another reason I focus on brokenness is that this book is written for Christians who are seeking to grow in their walk with Christ. I assume that most readers have, in some way, already come to grips with their guilt before God. And if you are part of Christ's kingdom, he has already atoned for your sins. You have already been justified on the basis of Jesus' life, death, and resurrection. You have bathed freely in God's grace.

What remains is your brokenness. Becoming a follower of Christ does not automatically mend it.

As Christians, we need to connect with our brokenness. We need to recognize the ways in which sin and rebellion have twisted our lives and damaged our relationships. We need to admit the ways we've become traitors to ourselves, hurt others, disowned God, and abused his creation. We need to acknowledge that even though parts of our lives may look well put together and under control, there are other ways in which we are still a mess. Some areas of our lives and relationships are still utterly broken. To the extent that we fail to own that we are broken, we deny that we need a Redeemer.

My message and the message of this book is that there *is* something to be done about our brokenness. We don't have to remain a crumpled mess lying paralyzed on the floor. Our lives may be *utterly* broken, but they are not *irretrievably* broken. There is a Redeemer—someone who stands ready and is more than capable to put our lives back together again.

We are ReCreatable.

The story that God is writing in the heavens and earth is a story of redemption. We were created to reflect his glory, and yes, we fell far short of our calling. But there is redemption. This includes forgiveness and the promise of eternal life; but redemption also provides for the curse to be reversed. Adam and Eve rejected their opportunity to embrace holiness, the truly human life. Jesus came to offer us a second chance to live well, as fully mature human beings.

On my office desk I keep a seashell shard. Most people who visit the beach pick up the largest, most beautiful, unbroken seashells they can find. Those are the ones they pack carefully in their luggage to take home and proudly display. But once, a man gave me this shard of a shell he had picked up on the beach. And I kept it. It stays right there next to my computer keyboard.

I pick up that seashell shard sometimes three or four times a day and turn it over and over again in my hand. After several years of handling it this way, it is now smooth, shiny, polished. I hold on to this seashell shard because it reminds me that I too am a shard—a broken person. All of us are. But we have a creator God who does not toss aside the broken pieces. He picks them up, treasures them, and redeems them.

Personal Reflection

1. What are some of the times in your life when you have felt most broken?
2. What are the ways in which your life feels broken at this moment?
3. Which of the three destructive attitudes (discontent, distrust, disregard) are you most aware of in your life?
4. Which of the four relationships (self, others, God, creation) feels most broken in your life right now?
5. In what ways would you most like to see God bring healing and redemption to your life as you work through this book?
6. Whom else do you know who might benefit from reading this chapter? Will you share it with him or her in some way?

Next Steps

1. Acknowledge to yourself, God, and at least one other person that you have some areas of brokenness in your life right now for which you would like to experience healing and redemption.

2. Identify one destructive attitude that you would like to eliminate from your life.
3. Identify one existing relationship that you would like to see restored to health.
4. Commit to making the attitude and relationship you chose a matter of regular prayer, trusting that God will bring healing.

Chapter 2

GLORY

[A person] is a fallen spirit whose only business in the present world is to recover from his fall, to regain that image of God wherein he was created.

—John Wesley

We live in a disposable culture. Look around your home sometime and consider how many of the things you see you still expect to have on hand twenty years from now—or even five years from now. Our cell phones and laptop computers are designed to last two or three years at most. If you get five years out of a TV, you're fortunate. Cars are designed to fail after about 100,000 miles. Furniture, which used to be passed down through the generations, we now expect to exchange at least three or four times over the course of a lifetime. If something breaks, we simply throw it away and buy a new one.

When my kids were really little, they thought that Daddy could fix anything. They would bring me a broken toy, fully expecting that I could make it like new again. They learned better; Dad has a degree in theology. Soon it became, well, if Dad can't fix it, Grandpa probably can. That mantle fits him much better than it does me.

It seems that we are born with the desire to have things fixed rather than to throw them away. At least, we know that's best. And there is a unique appeal about something that has been restored to its original condition, whether it's a classic car, a musical instrument, a downtown building, or a family's home.

When God's world was broken—when sin tore heaven and earth apart—he didn't throw it away and start all over again. Instead, he began to redeem and restore it, to make it into a new creation. When humanity rebelled against God, humanity itself became broken. But God didn't destroy the human race; instead, he set about to restore it—to create a new, redeemed humanity.

God's great plan—the story he is writing in the world—is to bring all things in heaven and on earth together under the King, Jesus Christ (Eph. 1:10). When God created the heavens and the earth, they were totally and completely meshed together, so that God in heaven lived with humanity, and Adam and Eve lived in the presence of God, walking with him in the garden each day. The greatest tragedy that ever occurred was the sin of Adam and Eve, which ripped heaven and earth apart. Even though God is still very near to us and active in our lives, sin created a barrier so that humanity no longer had free access to God the way we did in the garden.

But God's plan since that day has been to fix that which was broken, to put heaven and earth back together again, so that we can once again live in the paradise God originally intended us to live in and experience genuine peace and fellowship with God and one another. And the great news is that God has already begun the work of putting heaven and earth back together again through Jesus Christ. He has already begun the work of new creation. And even now we can experience little glimpses of God's new creation. We can experience glorious moments of life in God's kingdom. And we typically find this when two or three or more followers of Jesus Christ are gathered together doing the kinds of things that Jesus called us to do.

Glory in the Garden

If you want to understand God's plan of redemption for the world and your life, you have to go back before the brokenness to try to understand what God intended when he began this project. You have to go back, in other words, to the garden of Eden. The garden was God's special gift to the first man and woman. It was both a home and a temple—a place where they could meet God as he visited them there. But while it certainly was paradise, it was not the sum total of his plan for them. When God created Adam and Eve in his image and gave them the garden, he provided everything they needed; but he didn't give them everything all at once. He gave them his glory, but he also gave them a calling: to bear his image into every part of his creation.

Diminishing Chaos

When God created the heavens and earth, he didn't create a perfect place. I know it sounds wrong, but stick with me. What God actually did was to create a place that had the *potential* for perfection. If the author of Genesis is to be believed (and I think he is), God's modus operandi is not to create something fully formed, perfect as soon as the creative word leaves his mouth. Instead, God seems to prefer to create the raw materials and then shape them into something special. Maybe it's the craftsman in him. Remember how the Genesis account of creation reads: "In the beginning, God created the heavens and the earth. The earth was without form and void, and darkness was over the face of the deep. And the Spirit of God was hovering over the face of the waters" (1:1–2).

At the moment God created the earth, it looked nothing like what you see when you look out your window each morning. God created the raw materials, and then he embraced the chaos and began to shape and craft it into something extraordinary. First, he introduced light, then an atmosphere and dry land. He made a sun and a moon. Then God added the creatures of the sea and the air and the land. Finally, and only after all of this work was done, God created man. The pattern of God's creative activity in Genesis 1 was to create the raw materials and then to slowly bring order and beauty to the chaos.

Pocket of the Kingdom

Even at this point in the creation story, we should not think of the earth as a perfect, beautiful paradise. There was still more work to be done. After creating the man—and apparently before creating the woman—God carved out a place for them to live. That's right. It seems that the wild and wonderful earth that God created was not fully inhabitable until he invested the additional time and effort to cultivate a small corner of it—the garden of Eden (Gen. 2:8). He planted trees, formed rivers, and generally provided everything the man and woman would need for a satisfying life. He told them that they would have to take care of the garden and avoid eating from one specific tree.

God's gift to Adam and Eve was one small corner of the earth where everything was as it should be. It surely was as beautiful as any place you can imagine, and within it, there was nothing but peace and harmony—with self, one another, God, and his creation. It was like a pocket of the kingdom where God was King and his rule was undisputed.

Expanding the Boundaries

Outside the garden, things were different. God had cultivated one small patch of earth, making it inhabitable for Adam and Eve, but there was still yet more work to be done. The rest of the earth needed to be subdued, tamed, and cultivated for human life. It still needed to be brought under the dominion of the King. But it was not God's intention to do that work himself. God gave them the model—the garden of Eden—and then told them to go and do likewise: "Be fruitful and multiply and fill the earth and subdue it and have dominion over the fish of the sea and over the birds of the heavens and over every living thing that moves on the earth" (Gen.1:28). God gave them a pocket of the kingdom where everything was as it should be and then commanded them to expand the boundaries until the whole earth was brought under their dominion and thus into his kingdom.

This, as much as anything, is what I think it means that humanity was created in God's image. God's glory is demonstrated by his dominion over the whole of reality. He was not selfish with his glory but decided to share it with humanity. He gave us the privilege and the responsibility to be image-bearers, glory-bearers. The glory is not our own; we can only reflect his glory.

Restoring the Glory

The story God is writing in the heavens and earth is one of redemption; or to put it another way, it's one of glory forfeited and re-gifted. We have reached again the starting place of chapter one, but hopefully now with a richer understanding of what was broken and what was lost. God shared his glory with humanity, giving us the privilege and opportunity to reflect his glory by being kings and rulers over his creation. And we flubbed it up.

Falling Short of the Glory

Adam and Eve were given an amazing opportunity, and they forfeited their calling. God tasked them with reflecting his image—bearing his glory—to the ends of the earth. But before they ever set foot out of the garden, they had already rejected his plan. They marred God's holy image in them and fell short of their calling to reflect God's glory.

In his letter to the Romans, Paul described the plight of all humanity with these words: "For all have sinned and fall short of the glory of God" (Rom. 3:23). Another way of saying it is that we have all followed in Adam and Eve's footsteps. While we have not had exactly the same opportunity that the first man and woman had, neither have any of us been more faithful. In our own way, each of us has had the opportunity to reflect the glory of a holy God in a certain place and among particular people. Yet, apart from Christ, our lives have been characterized more by sin and rebellion than by God's glory and holiness. Each of us, in our own way, is guilty of bringing additional brokenness into the world.

Rescued, Not Abandoned

When the first man and woman received the gift of the garden, there was perfect harmony. The Hebrew word is *shalom* (peace), a deep sense of everything being right with the world. The man and woman experienced an intimate relationship with God, who, in some way beyond our understanding, walked in the garden with them on a regular basis. The man and woman had a perfectly healthy and whole relationship with one another. And they lived in perfect harmony with all of creation, taking care of and exercising responsibility over the birds, animals, and all creation without abusing or exploiting them.

Just imagine a life where nothing is broken, where everything works the way it should. This is the world God gave us—the world that was broken the moment when humanity chose to rebel against God. When Adam and Eve gave in to the temptation to choose their own way, to rule their own lives, they introduced sin and evil into God's creation, and with it, all brokenness and suffering.

God could have chosen at that moment to scrap the whole project, to send it to the trash dump, to destroy it by fire. He did not. Instead He said, "I created this, and I can fix it." Instead of pitching out his creation, he chose to recycle it. Instead of destroying humanity, he decided to redeem and restore us. He chose to deal with the problem of sin and rebellion and to bring all things in heaven and earth under the reign of a wise and benevolent King, one who would succeed where Adam and Eve had failed. The Hebrew Torah, in the Old Testament, tells the story of God choosing a man, Abraham, and making him into a nation, Israel, through whom he could prepare the world to receive its one true King. The one thing Abraham had going for him was the one thing Adam and Eve (and later Israel) lacked: he trusted God (Gen. 15:6; Rom. 4:3).

A New Kind of Humanity

At Mount Sinai, God made a covenant with Abraham's family that he would be their God and they would be his people (Exod. 20). As long as they kept the covenant, they would experience God's presence and blessing. But if they rejected him and his Law, they would come under God's judgment (Deut. 28). The problem that came up repeatedly throughout the history of Israel was that they were utterly incapable of keeping their covenant with God; it was as if they were infected with a disease that turned their hearts away from God. They were children of Abraham, but even more, they were children of Adam and Eve, and they followed in their parents' rebellious footsteps.

Eventually God, through the prophets, promised that one day he would create a new kind of humanity (Jer. 31:33; Heb. 8:10; 10:16). This new race of people would be healed of the disease that had been passed down from Adam and Eve. They would be able to follow God's Law because it would be engraved on their hearts.

Pockets of the Kingdom

The way that God went about creating this new kind of humanity was similar in many ways to the opportunity he created for the first man and woman. He created a new pocket of the kingdom and commanded its members, in a sense, to be fruitful and multiply and to fill the earth and subdue it, bringing everything under the dominion of its King (Matt. 28:18–20). The difference is that the first time around, he empowered Adam and Eve to rule the world and reflect his glory throughout creation. When it came time to redeem humanity and reverse the curse brought on by Adam and Eve's failure, he entrusted this responsibility to one who he knew would not fail him—his true Son, Jesus Christ.

Jesus Is Lord and Redeemer

Jesus did what neither Adam and Eve nor Israel seemed capable of doing: he lived a life of perfect obedience and faithfully fulfilled his responsibility to reflect God's glory to all creation. God glorified Jesus, just as he had shared his glory with Adam; but Jesus was up to the task. By his holy life, sacrificial death, and glorious resurrection, Jesus provided the opportunity for men and women to be freed from their slavery to sin and death and to participate in a new kingdom.

Jesus travelled around first-century Galilee announcing that the kingdom of God was about to appear. The way to participate in it was to repent of all opposing commitments and allegiances and to embrace him as King and Lord (Matt. 4:17, 23). He welcomed all regardless of history, culture, status, or station in life, and he offered all the opportunity for redemption—to experience healing in their broken lives, to be put back together again.

A Circle of Faith

Initially, Jesus found a handful of faithful men and women to embrace his message and submit themselves to his lordship. He formed a small group of men and women who sat at his feet to learn from him (Matt. 4:18–22). Within this community or fellowship, Jesus began to teach them about the ways of the kingdom. They learned from the Master what it meant to be a true human being, one who genuinely reflects the glory of God in every relationship—with self, others, God, and his creation (Matt. 5:1–7:28). This little group of disciples became the place where and the means by which Jesus taught his followers what it meant to be a part of this new kind of humanity.

Within this circle, the disciples learned what it meant to be forgiven and redeemed. They learned what it meant to experience healing and reconciliation in all of their relationships. They began to taste life the way God intended it to be lived, which is what holiness is really about. They learned to follow Jesus in such a way that it became second nature. And they learned from the Master how to teach this way of life to others.

Expanding the Circles

It certainly did not happen right away. Before he returned to heaven, Jesus left his disciples with a commission to expand their little pocket of the kingdom—to multiply it—so that others too would have the opportunity to experience redemption and participate in this new way of being human, reflecting God's glory. Jesus told them, "'All authority in heaven and on earth has been given to me. Go therefore and make disciples of all nations, baptizing them in the name of the Father and of the Son and of the Holy Spirit, teaching them to observe all that I have commanded you. And behold, I am with you always, to the end of the age'" (Matt. 28:18–20).

But it didn't happen right away.

Jesus had instructed his disciples to wait at Jerusalem for the Holy Spirit to empower them for their mission. And wait they did. Then Pentecost came, and they were filled with the Holy Spirit and preached the gospel, and many embraced Jesus as Lord and Redeemer. At least in Jerusalem. It seems the disciples were very comfortable in their local pocket of the kingdom and so were reluctant to take the show on the road.

Eventually, the disciples' influence in Jerusalem grew to the point that the authorities began getting nervous. As a result, they started making life difficult for those who followed Jesus, throwing some in jail and even having a few of them killed. Finally, things got bad enough that the disciples started to scatter. And wherever they went, in every city, they established new pockets of the kingdom, communities of people who were devoted to the way of Jesus.

Your community of faith, whether big or small, is a direct descendent of one of these early pockets of the kingdom, made up of those who were faithful to the message and mission of Jesus.

Glory Flooding the Earth

More than 600 years before Jesus arrived in Galilee, the prophet Habakkuk offered this vision of the future: "For the earth will be filled with the knowledge of the glory of the Lord as the waters cover the sea" (Hab. 2:14).

And we are the glory-bearers. Imagine that.

An unknown pastor, writing to a persecuted church within a few decades after Jesus' death, resurrection, and ascension, said that Jesus was "crowned with glory and honor because of the suffering of death, so that by the grace of God he might taste death for everyone." At the same time, this pastor acknowledged that even though Jesus is Lord, "we do not yet see everything in subjection to him." He is delaying the final consummation of the kingdom in hopes of "bringing many sons to glory" (Heb. 2:8–10).

God granted humanity a wonderful gift: he shared his glory with us so that we could bear his image into all creation. We fell short of his glory, but he is giving us a second chance. Through his Son Jesus, we can receive forgiveness and redemption, along with a new opportunity to bear his image and reflect his glory. "How shall we escape if we neglect such a great salvation?" (Heb. 2:3).

Take up the call to be a glory-bearer.

Personal Reflection

1. What do you think it would look like to have a small corner of the earth where everything is as it should be?
2. In what ways have you seen God's glory reflected in the earth? In other people? In relationships?
3. What is it that currently keeps you from reflecting God's glory in your life? In your relationships?
4. In what ways have you followed in Adam and Eve's footsteps? How have you introduced brokenness into your world?
5. Do you know anyone, or have you ever known anyone, whom you would consider a glory-bearer? What was that person like?

6. Have you ever participated in a pocket of the kingdom? If so, what was it like? If not, what do you think it would be like?

Next Steps

1. Pay attention to the ways you see God's glory reflected in yourself, in others, and in his creation. Consider keeping a journal of your observations.

2. Make it a practice to acknowledge to God, yourself, and others that Jesus is your Lord and Redeemer. Let that truth begin to shape your life and behavior.

3. If you are not doing so already, seek to be a part of a pocket of the kingdom—of a group of people who acknowledge Jesus as Lord and Redeemer and are committed to helping one another learn to reflect his glory.

4. Begin praying for God to transform you so that more and more you reflect his glory in your life and relationships.

Chapter 3

INTERSECTION

The Bible's aim, as I read it, is not the freeing of the spirit from the world. It is the handbook of their interaction.
—Wendell Berry

In December 2002, my wife Debbie and I welcomed into the world our third child, Ethan Ray.

Just a few months into her pregnancy, Debbie's doctor discovered that Ethan had a lower urinary bladder obstruction that, left unattended, would prevent his lungs from forming properly and cause his kidneys to shut down. He also told us that there were a handful of surgeons in the country who had experienced success in doing an in utero procedure to open the obstruction. He immediately connected us with a surgeon in Tampa, and within a couple of days, we were walking into a hospital in Tampa for a pre-op consultation. Unfortunately, our hopes were quickly dashed, as the initial examination indicated that Ethan's kidneys were already beginning to shut down, like a switch had been flipped that couldn't be reversed.

Four months later, early on the morning of our tenth wedding anniversary, Debbie and I held Ethan in our arms for the first and only time. He stayed with us about seventy-five minutes. His older sisters and his grandparents held him and loved him. And then we had to say goodbye much too soon.

A couple of months later, I was in Sky Harbor International Airport in Phoenix on a layover on the way home from leading a workshop in southern California. As I sat waiting for my flight, I looked up from my book and inadvertently made eye contact with a baby boy who immediately reminded me of Ethan. It only lasted a moment, and it's hard to describe what I felt. It wasn't sadness; it was more like an overwhelming sense of Ethan's presence, as if Ethan were telling me he was safe and secure. As if for one brief moment, heaven and earth had intersected, and I had been given the chance to see my son again. I'm just telling you how it felt.

From one perspective, there's nothing extraordinary about seeing a baby boy at the airport. But for me at the time, there was something transcendent in that brief moment. Something of heaven touching earth. Later, flying through the air on the last leg of my journey, I remember feeling that Ethan was so close—and yet so far away. And the earlier sense of transcendence eroded into a bittersweet sadness.

There's something about flying through the sky that makes you feel close to heaven—to God and those who have gone on before you. And yet at the same time, it somehow emphasizes that you're not quite there.

If you pay attention, life is full of such momentary intersections between heaven and earth.

The extraordinary thing is, the Bible teaches that *you* are the kind of person who can facilitate such intersections for others. And yet, most of the time, like a tiny baby in an airport, you won't be aware that it's happening.

God's Neighborhood

If you're ever wondering what kind of neighborhood God would live in, take a good look at yourself—because God lives in you. Or at least that's where he wants to make a home for himself.

Heaven May Be Closer Than You Imagined

In the beginning God created the heavens and the earth. Earth is where we live, and heaven has generally been understood to be the place where God lives.

If you're like most people, you've imagined heaven to be a faraway place that you could never reach or find on your own. But Christians didn't learn this belief from the Bible. It actually fits much better with Greek philosophy and mythology than it does with biblical Christianity.

From its very beginning, the Bible suggests that heaven is much nearer than we have imagined. The story of heaven's creation is found in Genesis 1:6–8, where it's described not as a faraway place but as something that sounds a lot like the earth's atmosphere. In verse 7, God made an "expanse" above the earth. Some of the water he left on the earth, while some of the water he placed above the expanse.

In other words, we have lakes, rivers, and oceans that provide water for all of our earthly needs. We have an "expanse" that includes our breathable air. And then above that, God placed a storehouse of water that could be released as needed. The author of Genesis teaches that God eventually released the waters above the expanse in judgment rather than provision (Gen. 6–8). And now, of course, we have a sustainable water cycle where surface waters move freely between earth and sky—evaporation and precipitation.

But here's the point: the expanse that God created, in which the rains and snows are prepared for us, God called "heaven." In other words, we may be standing on earth, but we're walking (and sometimes flying) through heaven itself. If the author of Genesis is to be believed (and I think he is), heaven is not so far away as you might imagine. It's in the air you breathe.

The Rupture of Heaven and Earth

When we say that God lives in heaven, we're using an anthropomorphism (speaking of God as if he were a human being).

God doesn't live *anywhere*; everywhere lives in God.

But people have always found it helpful to think of God as living somewhere, and the Bible encourages us to think of God as living in heaven—again, meaning the atmosphere, the air we breathe. When Adam and Eve walked in the garden, they walked with God, and he visited them there.

But the fall (the man and woman's first rebellion against God) seems to have somehow ruptured the relationship between heaven and earth. When you think about this, you might have to work hard to remember that we're using words to describe something that in many ways is beyond our understanding. But after the fall, God no longer walked the earth the way he once did.

He didn't abandon it.

He didn't withdraw his claim over it.

But things were different. Very different.

It was as if a veil had been pulled between heaven and earth, preventing us from experiencing God like he intended. Maybe you have personal experience with that veil.

Piercing the Veil

Still, there have been times when the veil between heaven and earth has been pierced or momentarily lifted.

Think of the story of Jacob's ladder (Gen. 28:10–17). Jacob had outwitted his brother and deceived his father to acquire something that didn't belong to him—his family's birthright. His brother was so incensed that Jacob's life was in danger, so his mother and father sent him off to the land where Abraham's family lived, the land that Abraham left when he followed God's call. One night on the way, Jacob slept under the stars with a rock for a pillow. As he slept, he had a dream about a ladder with its feet on earth and its top extending to heaven. Angels were going up and down the ladder between Jacob and heaven. And God was at the top of the ladder, calling down to Jacob.

The remarkable thing about the ladder was not its height; Scripture doesn't say it was an unusually tall ladder. The remarkable thing was that it bridged two dimensions—the visible and the invisible, the seen and the unseen, the place where God lives and the place where we live, heaven and earth.

There is also the story of Elisha's servant when he was frightened by the Syrian armies that had surrounded the city. Elisha prayed and asked God to open his servant's eyes so he could see. "So the Lord opened the eyes of the young man, and he saw, and behold, the mountain was full of horses and chariots of fire all around Elisha" (2 Kings 6:15–17). These armies, the heavenly hosts, were there all the time, just beyond sight; it's just that human beings were not capable of seeing them without assistance. They inhabited another dimension, yet they were inextricably linked to the events playing out on earth.

Or think of the transfiguration where the inner circle of disciples was given the privilege of seeing their friend Jesus conversing face-to-face with two people who were at that moment inhabiting heaven (Matt. 17:1–9; Mark 9:2–8; Luke 9:28–36). They were not breathless from their journey; heaven is right here with us, if only we have eyes to see.

And, oh yeah, there's the time when Moses and seventy-three close friends had dinner with God on a mountain (Exod. 24:9–12). Did you catch that one in Sunday school? Heaven is not far away. It's in the very air you breathe.

The Celtic Christians of northern Ireland talked about "thin places"—places on earth where the veil separating heaven and earth seems somehow thinner, heaven more accessible. At such places, they thought you were more likely to experience God. It sounds superstitious to our modern ears. But consider this: Have you ever been in a place where you felt you could sense the presence of God in a palpable way? Even if the thought seems primitive today, it's based on a biblical, Hebrew way of thinking.

Heaven is very near to us and sometimes, at significant moments, makes itself known to us.

Now that you're inviting God to dwell in you (or at least considering making the invitation), let's take a look at some of the other places where God has lived.

Sanctuary

The Hebrew idea that heaven and earth are intertwined and intersecting, not surprisingly, goes back to the beginning.*

The Garden as Temple

God carved out a place for the first man and woman to live where everything was just as it should be. In the last chapter, I mentioned that the garden of Eden was both a home and a temple, because it

---

*As with so much in this book, this section has been heavily influenced by N. T. Wright's presentation of the material. You can find his material on the subject in N. T. Wright, *After You Believe: Why Christian Character Matters* (New York: HarperCollins, 2010), chapter 3.

was the place where Adam and Eve met God. The author of Genesis described the garden in a way that, for its first readers, might have evoked an image of the temple.* It was an enclosed sanctuary, with only one entrance that faced east. We know this because later a single cherubim was placed at the entrance to protect the tree of life (Gen. 3:24). Maybe God grew a hedge around the boundary of the garden to separate the chaos outside from the paradise inside. The word *paradise* is actually derived from a Persian word that means "royal park." The garden was a place set aside for the King and his servants to live, work, play, and worship.

The garden was also the source of a river, which parted and became four rivers. It is interesting that John's vision of the New Jerusalem in the book of Revelation also contains a river. He describes its "river of the water of life, bright as crystal, flowing from the throne of God and of the Lamb through the middle of the street of the city; also, on either side of the river, the tree of life with its twelve kinds of fruit, yielding its fruit each month. The leaves of the tree were for the healing of the nations" (Rev. 22:1–2).

John's tree of life imagery also comes from the description of the garden of Eden (Gen. 2:9). This tree is also thought to have been the inspiration for the golden candlestick with seven branches that was used in tabernacle and temple worship. The tree of the knowledge of good and evil finds its counterpart in the Law, which was stored in the ark of the covenant in both the tabernacle and the temple. The gold and onyx mentioned in connection with the garden are natural resources that were used to adorn the priests and the temple itself. They also feature in the description of the New Jerusalem (Rev. 21:11–21).

---

*Gordon J. Wenham, *Genesis 1–15*, Word Biblical Commentary (Waco, TX: Word, 1987), 61–66.

Overall, the impression we get is that the garden of Eden was the original sanctuary of God which inspired the later biblical sanctuaries—the tabernacle, the temple, and the New Jerusalem.

The Intersection of Heaven and Earth

The garden of Eden represents the one time and place where heaven and earth were fully and completely enmeshed, woven together with no separation. In the garden, heaven and earth were not two separate entities, but two sides of a single fabric. They were two pieces of a completed puzzle.

The garden of Eden was the place where God and humanity existed in perfect harmony. God regularly walked with Adam and Eve in the cool of the day (Gen. 3:8).

God. Walked. With Adam and Eve.

And no one thought it was strange or unusual. No one was amazed. When God appeared, it was not a miracle. It was just the way things were back then and there. It was the way God created the heavens and earth to function, so that there was easy communication and fellowship between the two. The strange thing would not have been for heaven to show up, but for heaven to be absent.

Frayed Fabric

Unfortunately, this remarkable set of circumstances would not long survive. One of the tragic consequences of the sin of Adam and Eve was that heaven and earth—or more precisely, what heaven and earth represented: God and humanity—were violently ripped apart. The fabric was torn and frayed.

To put it another way, a veil was drawn between heaven and earth, separating heaven and making its activities off-limits and invisible to inhabitants of the earth.

After the fall, humanity no longer had immediate access to the Creator. They no longer enjoyed free and easy communion with him. Adam and Eve were ejected from the sanctuary and prevented from returning.

The sanctuary itself was guarded for a time, and then, presumably, left to be engulfed and destroyed by its wild, untamed surroundings.

God's dwelling, sadly, was no longer with man.

Holy Hill

Though Adam and Eve were thrust from both their sanctuary and their fellowship with God, God was not without mercy. The Old Testament is full of examples where God, at certain times and places, withdrew the veil and connected directly with those who were faithful to him. Think of God instructing Noah to build the ark, making a covenant with Abraham, wrestling with Jacob, giving Joseph the ability to interpret dreams, speaking to Moses from a bush, and putting on a multi-media event for the Hebrew people at Mount Sinai. There are many more examples. Though in a sense God withdrew behind a veil, he has never left us alone in the world. His mercy caused him to continue to reach out to us from beyond the veil.

God's Dwelling Place

Eventually, God chose to give his people another sanctuary, though this one was much more limited and closely regulated. After making a covenant with the Hebrew people at the foot of Mount Sinai, God met with Moses and gave him instructions for a portable tabernacle (Exod. 25–30). This tent became the center of worship for the Hebrew people, and it featured a visual representation of God's presence—a cloud by day and a pillar of fire by night (Exod. 13:17–22; 40:38).

When the tabernacle was put up for the first time, "the cloud covered the tent of meeting, and the glory of the Lord filled the tabernacle. And Moses was not able to enter the tent of meeting because the cloud settled on it, and the glory of the Lord filled the tabernacle" (40:34–35). God's glory, which once lived in the garden of Eden, was given a new home. Just as God gave Adam and Eve the responsibility to reflect his glory throughout the world, that responsibility now rested on the nation of Israel.

Once the people of Israel took possession of the Promised Land, they eventually wanted to give God a more permanent residence. King David made known his desire to build a permanent temple on a prominent hill in Jerusalem. God approved the idea, but he told David to leave it for his son Solomon to build when he became king.

Since that time, two temples have stood on that mountain. The first, built by Solomon, was eventually destroyed in 586 B.C. when Jerusalem was besieged and conquered by the Babylonian Empire. The second was built by Zerubbabel after Cyrus, king of Persia, ended the Jewish exile. It was later renovated and expanded by King Herod just before the time of Christ. This second temple was destroyed by the Romans in A.D. 70.

The mountain on which the temple stood is still considered one of the holiest places in all the world. All three of the world's major religions claim it as part of their heritage. It has long been and probably always will be a major source of contention in the conflict between Arabs and Israelis.

Access to God

The thing about a temple is that it offers access that can't be found anywhere else.

When I was working as an event planner, signing contracts with hotels for large annual conferences, salespeople sometimes made me feel as if I had access that other people didn't have. Once I was negotiating a contract with a large hotel in a trendy city on the West Coast. While I was in town, the hotel made dinner reservations for me in its restaurant on the top floor, one of the highest-rated restaurants in the city.

When I arrived, several unhappy people were waiting in the lobby, and then came an announcement that the restaurant would be unable to open for some time due to unexpected circumstances.

But as I wondered how long I would have to wait, I heard the hostess call my name. After I introduced myself to her, she said, "I'll take you to your table now."

There I sat, alone in an empty restaurant with a gorgeous 360-degree view of the city at dusk, and while others were turned away, I was served a sumptuous, five-course meal. It was the first and only time such a thing has happened to me.

Soon after I began eating, my hotel contact showed up at my table and said, "How nice that we reserved the entire restaurant for you!" Then he explained that the chef had been unexpectedly unavailable, and they were scrambling to open the restaurant at all that evening. But they had managed to bring in a chef from one of their other properties to ensure that I enjoyed my dinner on time.

Of course, I had no illusion that it was about me; it was all about the money that my organization represented for the hotel. Still, it felt to me like unprecedented access. Maybe you've had similar experiences of special access—a backstage pass, a private tour, or a unique offer.

Both the tabernacle and the temple represented an even more extraordinary kind of access; they represented Israel's access to God.

When God was in his temple, the Israelites did not have to wonder where they could find him. They didn't have to question whether he would hear them. God kept office hours, so to speak. Scripture, especially the Psalms, has numerous examples of God's people looking toward the "holy hill" for help: "I lift up my eyes to the hills. From where does my help come? My help comes from the Lord, who made heaven and earth" (Ps. 121:1–2).

The Israelites knew that God's temple granted them access to their covenant God.

Forgiveness

In addition to representing the presence of God and access to him, both the tabernacle and the temple also symbolized the forgiveness of sins the Israelites could experience through the covenant. The major activity that took place at the temple was an elaborate system of animal and agricultural sacrifices.

While Christians have often thought such a system represented a way of earning salvation by works, that was never the intent and probably never entered the minds of the ancient Israelites. Their forgiveness was based on their being members of God's covenant with Israel. The sacrifices they offered were not a way of earning or gaining entrance to anything. Forgiveness was already theirs because they were already members of the covenant. The sacrifices were a way of maintaining their membership, so to speak, and ensuring that they were not removed from covenant consideration.

So the temple became a focal point for the forgiveness of sins, both small and large, and a way of maintaining their covenant relationship with God.

Temple on the Move

We've seen that the locus of God's presence has moved over time from the garden of Eden to the tabernacle to the temple in Jerusalem.

By the time Jesus arrived on the scene, there was more than one movement within Judaism that questioned whether God was in fact still "dwelling" at the second temple in Jerusalem. The Pharisees were critical of Herod's temple, which was run by powerful Saducean priests. (The Pharisees and Sadducees were the two major "parties" of Jewish public life in the first century.) And the Essenes did more than criticize the system; they completely withdrew from it, taking their families to live in the desert and wait for the arrival of the Messiah. They believed he would judge the current temple system and replace or rebuild it.

The Perfect Sacrifice

When Jesus arrived, he connected with some existing frustrations about the temple, but he created some additional frustrations too. At least once and maybe twice, Jesus entered the Jerusalem temple and created a disturbance, traditionally called the "cleansing of the temple" (Matt. 21:12–13; John 2:13–21). But more than a cleansing (the merchants went right back to their old ways as soon as he left the premises), Jesus was probably enacting a prophecy against the temple. He had knocked over a few tables, but God was going to do much worse than that in time. The Pharisees and Essenes would have loved it. The Sadducees, not so much. And the Sadducees were powerful people.

Jesus also told his critics that if they tore down the temple, he would rebuild it in three days. This was certainly another threat of judgment on the temple, but it was also more. The disciples later realized Jesus meant that his body would be destroyed on the cross, and that he would rise again in three days.

In other words, he was claiming that he had come to replace the temple with his own body.

The disciples would also later understand that through his death on the cross, Jesus offered the perfect sacrifice and thus made the temple system with all of its sacrifices obsolete. Those who were looking for all of the things that the temple offered—access to God's presence, forgiveness of sins, the opportunity for redemption, assurance of a place in the covenant—would now find those things in Jesus alone.

And you can find those same things in Jesus today.

The Body of Christ

But there is more. With the life, death, and resurrection of Jesus, God's glory and presence became localized again in yet another place—the body of Jesus Christ.

Shortly after his resurrection, Jesus ascended back to heaven, the invisible realm, to administer God's plan from the right hand of his throne. But it would not do for God to be left without representation on earth.

So Jesus gave his disciples the privilege and opportunity to *be* his body. And today, God's presence on earth is to be found in the body of Christ, the church.

A Temple of the Spirit

Another way of saying this is that you, as a member of the body of Christ, have become a temple of the Holy Spirit (1 Cor. 6:19). Too often the church has reduced this amazing truth to a concern for taking care of our body or avoiding sin. While those things are important, they miss the point.

As a temple of the Holy Spirit, you have become a point of intersection between heaven and earth, a place where and a means by which people can, in some mysterious way, encounter God's presence. It is in the temple of the Holy Spirit where God's glory is revealed.

And as I mentioned before, most of the time, you'll be unaware that anything extraordinary is happening.

A few years ago, some of the leaders of our church were discussing what the kingdom would look like to a particular person for whom Anna was praying. Kenny gave a brilliant answer. He said that, for that person, the kingdom looks like Anna, because the Holy Spirit in Anna may be the only glimpse of God this person sees.

That's what the Bible means when it says that you are the temple of the Holy Spirit.

You are the temple, and therefore God dwells in you both as an individual and as part of the body of Christ. You are the temple, and therefore you are God's representative wherever you go. It is your calling to be the bearer of God's glory. In some mysterious way, you convey the presence of God on earth.

I have a friend who tells the story of a former seminary professor who would say the same thing every time my friend would go and visit him. He would say, "I know who sent you to me today. You look just like him." And of course, that was his way of saying, "You are the presence of Christ to me."

Most often, we'll be very much unaware of when we're conveying Christ to someone else in this way. We'll think that we are merely going about our ordinary business. If we try to be Christ for someone else, we're likely to completely mess it up. Nevertheless, we must be ready for such intersections. And the way to be ready for them is the subject of the rest of this book. We need to soak in Christ's presence so that others will see his reflection in our lives.

God's Presence Unleashed

The result of all of this is that we who are Christians have become "thin places." You, along with all other believers, are the place where and the means by which people can encounter the living God, experience his presence, and receive his offer of redemption. God's presence is no longer localized to a specific garden or country or hill, or even in a single person.

God's presence is unleashed and on the move wherever God's people are living out their calling to be the temple of the Holy Spirit.

Part of what it means to be God's temple, however, is to be sanctified, set aside for God's use, made holy. That's why part of our calling is to become authentically holy. If you are to reflect God's presence and glory wherever you go, you should be on your way to becoming the kind of person for whom following Jesus has become second nature. In other words, you must allow God to make you . . . holy.

Personal Reflection

1. What experiences in your life might represent an intersection of heaven and earth?
2. What are some of the places where you typically experience God's presence and peace?
3. Who in your life most naturally conveys God's presence to you?
4. What are some of the ways people have "been Christ to you," probably without even knowing it?
5. Has anyone ever told you that your presence in his (or her) life was especially meaningful to him? How might this show that you are a temple of the Holy Spirit?
6. How might your life need to change so that others more easily see Christ in you?

Next Steps

1. Identify at least one moment in your life when you felt that God "pierced the veil" for you. Find a concrete way—a journal

entry, a photograph, a song, a piece of artwork—to remember this experience so that you can recall it when necessary.

2. Determine at least one key place in your neighborhood or community where you seem to be able to connect with God. Make plans to visit that place at least once each week for the next couple of months.

3. Consider the people in your life in whom you see Christ. Is there a way to spend a bit more time with them? If so, make it happen on a regular basis.

4. Think about a person who always seems to be encouraged by your presence. Make plans to connect with that person on a regular basis.

Chapter 4

HOLY

God doesn't just forgive sin; he transforms sinners into Christ-
like figures and clothes them with Christ's righteousness.
—Miroslav Volf

When my daughter Lauren was three years old, she already knew what she wanted to be when she grew up. She wanted to be a dog. And not just any kind of dog. She wanted to be a fire dog.

Or, as she sometimes said, a dal-a-mation.

Many people lament that the church no longer seems to be producing disciples the way it should. Part of the problem, as far as I can see, is that we don't know what we want to be when we grow up. Or perhaps we've set our sights too low. We're not entirely sure what a fully mature disciple of Jesus really looks like.

It's not that we lack for examples. It's more that we don't know what we're looking for. Some people we look up to are actually not all that mature; others we overlook are mature beyond their years.

I'm increasingly convinced that being a fully mature disciple of

Jesus—becoming holy—is mostly about learning to live well. It's about living a life of Christlike faith, hope, and love. About learning to relate well with God, with others, and with God's creation. A life that's attractive to others. Else why would anyone care to listen when you tell them that Jesus is your Lord and Redeemer?

Please understand that what I have in mind is different from simply living a "good, moral life"—avoiding the big sins entirely and managing the little ones so that they don't get out of control. In fact, I'm not talking about "sin management" at all.* Christian holiness is not about a list of dos and don'ts. It doesn't mean never messing up, never doing anything wrong.

Holiness is more about always intending to get things right.

One thing I know for sure, you can't do it on your own. The power to live the way that I'm describing only comes by the transformation of the Holy Spirit. But that doesn't mean that it's automatic just because you're a Christian. Like the apostle Paul said, you have to work out your redemption (Phil. 2:12). And it sort of helps to know what you're shooting for.

Someone might raise an objection: "God wants me to do more than just live well. He called me to be a pastor." Great! How will you be a great pastor if you don't first learn to live well?

Has God called you to be a missionary? That's fantastic too. But you'll never be a great missionary if your life is out of whack.

The thing is, the more you allow Christ to put your life back together so that you really begin to live well, the more effective a servant of Christ you will be.

God has called you to be a fully mature follower of Jesus Christ—

---

*"Sin management" is a phrase that Dallas Willard uses in *The Divine Conspiracy* (San Francisco: HarperCollins, 1997), chapter 2.

to be holy. I'm still learning to do that too, but maybe we can learn together.

Mature Humanity

There is a way of reading the Bible that makes it all about heaven and hell and where you're going to be after you die.

Sometimes I've heard preachers who read the Bible this way focus on how great heaven is going to be and how much you're going to want to be there. Much more often I've heard them focus on how horrible hell is going to be and how much you're going to want to avoid it.

Fear is apparently better than hope at producing the kind of results those preachers want.

Those who want to avoid the stigma of being "hellfire and damnation" preachers are careful to focus much more on the cross and forgiveness than on heaven or hell. But the emphasis is often the same: the importance of punching your ticket for the right eternal destination.

Do that, and anything else, it seems, is a bonus.

This understanding of the Bible inevitably reduces Christianity to two primary behaviors: avoiding a way of life that will condemn you to hell and helping others learn how they can avoid hell as well.

I know, because I grew up in a tradition that often tended toward this view of Scripture. It is the kind of thinking that led to one of the crisis points of my faith.

This was probably fifteen years ago. I was pretty much finished with seminary except for writing my thesis. Though I had been through seemingly endless hours of Bible and theology classes in college and seminary, I had seen little to suggest that anything was more important than the two goals of avoiding hell and helping others do the same—although those objectives were usually communicated in a more positive way.

For many years, I had been preparing myself for a ministry of making heaven as attractive and hell as repulsive as I could, so that as many people as possible would make the right decision to follow Jesus.

And yet, on the brink of finishing my preparation for that ministry, it all began to have a hollow, tinny sound in my ears. Something didn't quite ring true.

I have not typically been the kind of guy to talk through these sorts of theological crises with others. It always seemed too risky, even with the closest of friends. Rather, I've been the kind who reads and thinks his way through such crises until he has a pretty good idea of where he's headed.

Eventually, I began to see that there is another way to read the Bible. While it is possible to read the Bible as if it is all about heaven and hell, you can only do so by minimizing or distorting some of the Bible's key themes and concerns.

What I began to see by reading people like N. T. Wright, Dallas Willard, Eugene Peterson, and Wendell Berry was that the Bible has much more to say about this life than the next. That this life matters beyond the one decision.

I began to give verses like this one their due: "God's goal is for us to become mature adults—to be fully grown, measured by the standard of the fullness of Christ" (Eph. 4:13 CEB).

So, God's goal for us is to become mature human beings.

Wow.

I don't think I ever quite got that message in any of the countless sermons I heard growing up. Maybe it was just my tone-deafness.

And while I very much like the translation of that verse I quoted above, it still misses the full impact of the Greek verse from which it is translated. What the Greek says is that God wants us to become the "perfect man." And that's not to discriminate against the women. The "perfect man" is Jesus, the prime example of the fully mature human being.

Whether male or female, God wants you to grow up to become like Christ.

Of course, I would never diminish the importance of "making a decision," and I absolutely believe that our eternal destinies are determined by our response to Christ.

But what I began to see is that it is possible to focus so much on the eternal destiny part that you miss out on God's goal for you—of becoming a fully mature human being. Of becoming the perfect man or woman. Of becoming like Jesus.

Here. Now.

In this chapter, and even more in the next section, we're going to explore together what it means to be a fully mature human being, a person who reflects Christ's glory in all his or her relationships—with God, with one another, with self, and with God's creation.

That's the thing. The fully mature human being is the one who is most at home within the world and among the people whom God created. The fully mature human being is the one whose character and way of life are a perfect fit for the eternal kingdom of God. That's what it means to be holy, set apart for God's purposes.

To Be Like Jesus

Many Christians don't know what they want to be when they grow up, but when it comes to the Bible, there is no question about our goal and example.

Our example is Jesus of Nazareth, the fully mature human being. And our goal is to be like him.

Some will say that this is too lofty a goal, even an unfair one, like asking the aspiring painter to be more like Rembrandt or the aspiring ballplayer to be more like Willie Mays. They will say that Jesus had the advantage of being God in human flesh. They will point out that we were born corrupt, with a fallen nature. That Jesus was different from us.

But that's the wrong perspective. That's to make Jesus somehow less than human. Jesus was 100 percent human being, and that means that whatever weaknesses and temptations we experience, he experienced too.

Some people get hung up because they think "being like Jesus" mostly means not messing up, not committing sins. But I seriously doubt that Jesus walked around Galilee thinking, "OK, yesterday was another day without sin. Don't blow it today." Maybe Jesus didn't spend a lot of time thinking about sinning or not sinning. Maybe he was too busy being himself. Maybe the greatest thing about Jesus wasn't what he lacked (sin), but what he was full of: faith, hope, and love.

We don't know at what point Jesus became aware of his true identity and calling. But we do know that, as a human being, he had the capacity to doubt that identity and calling. Otherwise, how can we make sense of the garden of Gethsemane? Yet at every step of the way, Jesus acted with *faith* in God the Father, who had declared his Son's identity to him at his baptism. And Jesus' faith was neither a foregone conclusion nor some fatalistic stab in the dark. He had immersed himself in the Scriptures and knew the story he was participating in.

Jesus believed that God would not abandon him to the grave but would raise him to new life and place him on the throne of God's eternal kingdom. He consistently acted in *hope* that a righteous God would do exactly what he said he would do.

And Jesus was best known for the *love* that he showed those with whom he related. He was always seeking to bring restoration and redemption to the broken lives and relationships of the people around him. Moreover, he said that people could know who his disciples are by the kind of love they show for one another.

Maybe Jesus wasn't sinless merely because he carefully avoided doing the wrong thing. Maybe Jesus was sinless because he was consumed with doing the right thing. His entire life was characterized by faith, hope, and love. And that is why he is our supreme example.

The apostle Paul certainly had Jesus in mind in Ephesians 4 when he described the fully mature human life. Here are four ways Paul urges us to embrace a fully mature life in the Spirit.

Walk Worthy

For many of us, when we read something in Scripture like Paul's challenge "to walk in a manner worthy of the calling to which you have been called" (Eph. 4:1), we immediately translate it into Ascetic. What I mean is, we assume that "walk worthy" is code language that means something like, "Don't mess up." But walking worthy isn't about avoiding sin; it's about reflecting God's glory with your whole life, "with all humility and gentleness, with patience, bearing with one another in love, eager to maintain the unity of the Spirit in the bond of peace" (v. 2).

Those aren't negative commands about things to avoid; they're mature attitudes to guide our relationships. Paul was describing the perfect man, Jesus, and his perfection was seen much more by what he did than by what he didn't do. You don't walk worthy by conquering sin; you walk worthy by embracing Christian faith, hope, and love. Victory over sin is a byproduct of the process of becoming more fully human.

Take Responsibility

God has uniquely gifted you for service in his kingdom. With maturity comes the confidence and focus to take on responsibility in the areas in which you are gifted. While you are probably capable of doing many things, find that one thing, or if you're especially blessed, maybe the two things that God is calling you to do—whether because of your skills, passion, connections, situation, or unique opportunities. Then, as hard as it is to do, put all those other things in the background and focus primarily on the thing God has uniquely gifted and called you to do. After all, imagine how much Jesus could have accomplished if he had done everything he was capable of doing! Instead, he chose the one thing only he could do and gave his life to accomplish it.

If you're having a hard time determining what God has gifted and called you to do, look for assistance from other mature Christians. God has specially gifted some people in the church to equip other Christians and prepare them for the ministry for which they have been gifted. And their equipping is part of what helps us to grow up into "the perfect man." The key thing is to be ready to take on responsibility, even if you're not absolutely sure you're gifted in a particular area. Many people have discovered their gifts after accepting the offer of a responsibility even though they had no idea they were gifted in that area. Such experimentation is often a great way to find your place within the body of Christ.

Speak the Truth in Love

Many people have no problem speaking the truth, no matter how much it hurts. They do it most naturally. Other people have no difficulty speaking with love, as if it's just a part of who they are. What demonstrates true maturity as a human being is the ability to speak the truth in love.

Speaking the truth in love is more than speaking the truth to someone you love. It is speaking the truth in a way that the person you love is able to hear and receive it. As we grow up in Christ, Paul says, this combination of courage and sensitivity is one of the hall-marks of a fully mature human being.

Clothe Yourself

Growing in maturity, Paul says, is like taking off a dirty set of clothes and putting on a clean set. And it's important to note that Paul doesn't assume that you're just going to get your new clothes dirty too; he expects that you'll have genuine victory over sin. But it requires making a conscious decision, in the power of the Spirit, to put off your old set of thoughts, attitudes, and behaviors and put on a brand new set patterned after God's image.

In other words, our new self is like Eve before the fall. Or like Jesus pretty much any time.

And as you consciously put on this new set of thoughts, attitudes, and behaviors, you'll discover that sin no longer has the same power in your life that it once did. Not that you'll never have to wrestle with it. And not that you'll never have a weak moment. But overall, there will be a definite and noticeable trend away from the old life and toward the new.

If it sounds like hard work, it is, but don't despair. Much more in part 2 of this book about how it all works. And don't forget that it's the Holy Spirit who lives in you who has the job of making the transformation happen.

Taking the Scary Out of Holy

Holiness is a scary topic for many people, and it need not be. The reason so many of us shy away from it is that we have a misconception about what it means to be holy.

As I understand it, Jewish ritual law had three categories: unclean, clean, and holy.

In ancient times, most people were considered "clean" at most times. This meant that they were free to interact in the community and participate in rituals of public worship.

But most everyone would also go through certain times, because of circumstances such as contact with a dead body or various bodily discharges, when they were considered "unclean." This wasn't necessarily an indication of sinfulness, only of a need to withdraw temporarily from participating in the community. Typically, they waited a prescribed amount of time and then participated in a ritual cleansing before connecting again with the community.

Most people at most times were clean, with temporary times of uncleanness.

The third category of Jewish ritual law included those who were considered holy. Holy, in this context, didn't mean *sinless* but *consecrated*, set apart for God's use and purposes.

The furniture in the temple was considered holy not because it was better furniture, but because it was set apart for use in God's service. The priests were considered holy not because they were better people but because they were consecrated for God's service.

Just like everyone else, priests occasionally became unclean. It didn't mean they could never again serve in the temple. They observed the period of uncleanness, participated in the ritual cleansing, and then resumed their service.*

The New Testament says that we are a kingdom of priests. Through the blood of Jesus Christ all who place their faith in him have been consecrated, set apart for his purposes.

That includes you.

---

*For more, see Gordon Wenham, *The Book of Leviticus*, New International Commentary on the Old Testament (Grand Rapids: Eerdmans, 1979), 18–23.

That doesn't mean that we all serve in a paid position in a church. Most of us don't and shouldn't. But it does mean that wherever you go and whatever you do, you represent him to the world. It means your life reflects his glory to some extent. It means your actions and interactions with others are characterized by faith, hope, and love, and by the fruit of the Spirit.

Holiness is not about a checklist of things to do and not to do, although I wouldn't want to completely discount the usefulness of checklists for learning a new way of life.

Holiness is much more about what we do than what we don't do. And it's more about who we're becoming than who we are today.

OK, so maybe that doesn't completely take the scary out of holy, but at least it puts the fear in its proper place. If you are a Christian, you have already been set apart. In one sense, you are already holy. What remains is for you to learn to live out that calling, to order your life so that God can be glorified in it. Growing in holiness is about learning to let God's glory be reflected in your whole life.

Why I Am Optimistic About Holiness

You may have noticed that I have a rather optimistic view of Christian holiness. I like to think of it as *realistic optimism*. I do not deny the continuing effects of humanity's choice to rebel against God nor the inherent brokenness of all human life.

However, I also believe that Christ's redemption is real.

And effective.

And for today.

There are plenty of pessimistic options available when it comes to Christian living. I like to joke with my Wesleyan and Baptist friends that Wesleyans believe we can and must be holy; Baptists and other more reformed types believe we must and *can't* be holy.

It's interesting to examine the reasons why we become pessimistic about the possibility of holy living. Some, in my opinion, are based on faulty exegesis; others, on inadequate psychology. I'll leave such arguments for another time and place. As I draw this first section of the book to a close, I want to focus on the reasons Christians should confidently and persistently seek to live a holy life—and expect to succeed.

I have already said that I believe holiness is more about what we do than what we don't do. Yes, the New Testament has a few lists of things we're to "put off." But the greater emphasis is on "putting on" faith, hope, love, and the fruit of the Spirit.

When Jesus was asked about the greatest commandment in the Law, he didn't choose a negative one, but a positive one: "You shall love the Lord your God with all your heart and with all your soul and with all your mind" (Matt. 22:37). Then he went on to add a second, equally positive one: "You shall love your neighbor as yourself" (v. 39).

We must stop thinking of the holiness God requires as the absence of sin and start thinking of it as embracing these positive commands. What we learn is that when we learn to love, for example, we are better equipped to avoid sinning against those we love—again, never perfectly (I'm a realistic optimist) but genuinely and in increasing measure.

Three reasons why we should confidently and optimistically pursue holiness:

God Demands It

There is one disputed passage (Romans 7) where on the surface Paul seems to be saying that it is normal for the Christian to be constantly in turmoil over sin. Outside of that single, beloved, disputed passage (by disputed, I mean that I do not think it means what some people think it means), the consistent testimony of the New Testament is that the normal Christian life is one of increasing holiness.

Christ's Redemption Purchased It

I am absolutely sympathetic to the objection that we human beings simply don't have it in us to be obedient to God's demands. However, the New Testament teaches us that Christ's redemption frees us from both the penalty *and* the power of sin. As a result, we are able to *not* sin. We are capable, through the death and resurrection of Jesus Christ, of living a redeemed life. Never perfect, but genuine and in increasing measure.

The Holy Spirit Empowers It

We are not left on our own to learn to reflect God's glory in all that we do. The Holy Spirit prompts, encourages, convicts, and empowers us to live a life worthy of our calling. Again, never perfect, but genuine and in increasing measure.

So, we have three indisputable witnesses—the Father, Son, and Holy Spirit—who testify that we can expect to make progress in living a life that reflects God's original intention for us when he created humanity.

I do not intend to say that it is easy (although I will suggest in the next section that over time it can become second nature). I do want to say that holiness is both possible and expected. It doesn't usually happen overnight. But if you are faithful, you can expect to look back in ten years and see how God is transforming you. And then ten years later, you'll see even more and different ways.

On the other hand, if you give in to the pessimism that tomorrow will be like today, and that in five or ten years you'll still have exactly the same struggles you're having today, you have little reason to expect such transformation to occur.

Pursue holiness and expect God to deliver. This is faith—believing that God will do what he says he will do.

"Now may the God of peace himself sanctify you completely, and may your whole spirit and soul and body be kept blameless at the coming of our Lord Jesus Christ. He who calls you is faithful; he will surely do it" (1 Thess. 5:23–24).

What to Do When You're Pessimistic About Holiness

Life is messy. Becoming a Christian doesn't eliminate the mess.

In fact, an argument could be made that becoming a Christian makes life *feel* messier.

Suddenly you can see the difference between what life can be and what life is right now, and you ache for a better way, but it seems always just out of your grasp.

While progress in holiness is certainly both possible and expected, that doesn't mean you will feel at every moment—or even most moments—as if you are growing and becoming more like Christ.

Some days (or weeks), you may feel like you're just the same as you've always been and ever will be. Sometimes you may feel as if it's all a loss, like you've sunk lower than you've ever been.

All of this is completely normal, and there are perfectly rational reasons why we sometimes feel this way. Here are a few practical steps you can take to get you through such times.

Be gracious with yourself. God's grace for you is deeper and wider than you can possibly imagine. Let God's grace constantly wash over you like a refreshing, cleansing stream.

Talk with a trusted person. This should be a person who can listen without being judgmental and give insight without being critical. Just talking through your struggles with someone you trust will give some much needed perspective.

Check your progress. Feelings can fluctuate with each day or week as you navigate life's peaks and valleys. Check the progress you're making, but not against yesterday or last week. Look back over the past year or five years. Measure your growth over the long term instead of the short term. If you can't see any growth over the long term, ask others to help you see where you've grown. Then consider what intentional changes you might need to make in order to nurture growth in the future.

Participate in Christian community. Some people tend to withdraw from their faith community during more pessimistic times. But these are the times when you need your brothers and sisters in Christ more than ever. Borrow freely from the faith and wisdom that is stored within your Christian community.

Listen for God's voice. Consider what God might be trying to say to you. None of us are perfect; we all have plenty of room to grow. Sometimes pessimism can signal that you're coming to a place in your journey where you'll need to make some changes. It can even be an indication that you're making more progress than you think; you just have to pull together the courage you need to take the next steps.

Pursue wisdom. The Bible consistently lays out two pathways: a pathway toward wise, godly, mature living and a pathway that leads to destruction. Even when you *feel* pessimistic about holiness, continue to seek wisdom and to pursue the pathway that leads to life. It just makes sense to do so.

Remember that the pathway to holiness is a lifelong journey. There will be times when you feel the journey is too long, times when you need to stop and rest. There will be unfortunate detours and times when you want to give up and go home.

Take care of yourself, and let others take care of you too.

Then make yourself get back out on the road, and keep your eyes on the destination.

Personal Reflection

1. Do you tend to be more optimistic or pessimistic about holiness? Why do you think this is?
2. How would you describe or define a fully mature human being?
3. What are some of the key ways that you need to grow into your maturity as a person of faith, hope, and love?
4. What do you think about the idea that holiness is more about what you do than what you don't do?
5. What are you doing in order to discover or embrace the one or two things God has gifted you to do? What are your next steps?
6. What are some of the key ways you have grown in holiness over the past year? Five years? More?

Next Steps

1. Do a personal inventory of the ways you have grown in the past year, five years, and ten or more years.
2. Choose at least one way you would like to see yourself grow in maturity in the next year.
3. Consider what a plan might look like to "put on" maturity in the area you chose in question 2, then make a plan.
4. Talk with a pastor or other trusted person about the ways you think you might be gifted to serve in the kingdom. Ask what insights he or she might have about your gifts and calling.

Part Two

BY LIVING WELL

This life, therefore, is
not righteousness,
    but growth in righteousness,
not health,
    but healing,
not being,
    but becoming,
not rest,
    but exercise.
We are not yet what we shall be,
    but we are growing toward it.
The process is not yet finished,
    but it is going on.
This is not the end,
    but it is the road.
All does not yet gleam in glory,
    but all is being purified.
                              —Martin Luther

Chapter 5
SUSTAINABLE

You don't think your way into a new kind of living. You live your
way into a new kind of thinking.

—Henri Nouwen

One of the hesitations I've had about writing a book on discipleship and the Christian life is the fear that my voice will merely be added to the many voices that already make many Christians feel like they're not good enough, not doing enough, and never will measure up to the expectations of being a disciple of Jesus.

For quite some time, I've had a growing suspicion that the Christian life as it is taught in the modern church is unlivable. Or at least it's unsustainable. Our hope and joy are robbed by unreasonable expectations, unnecessary stress, and inevitable guilt and shame.

There are too many voices, too many "experts," and too much well-meaning advice about the life of a disciple. We're supposed to be actively involved in Bible study, prayer, worship, small groups, church meetings, church fellowships, evangelism projects, service projects, missions projects, community groups. We're supposed to spend every free moment with our family yet be actively engaged in the community. We're supposed to give all of our money away to help the needy yet stay out of debt. We're supposed to love our neighbor, but probably there's a good chance we should be on the mission field instead.

No one ever tells us how we're supposed to do it all or fit it all in.

And we feel defeated. And guilty.

And here's the dirty little secret. You can do all of the above . . . and still not be a disciple.

By contrast, Jesus said, "Come to me, all who labor and are heavy laden, and I will give you rest. Take my yoke upon you, and learn from me, for I am gentle and lowly in heart, and you will find rest for your souls. For my yoke is easy, and my burden is light" (Matt. 11:28–30; see also 1 John 5:3).

Do you think it's safe to assume that if the yoke paralyzes you and the burden weighs you down, then it's not Jesus? I think that's safe to say. What Jesus describes is a more sustainable discipleship, a sustainable holiness.

I'm not sure how I missed it for so many years. But here's what I'm after:

Following Jesus is mostly about learning to live well—to become a fully mature human being.

It doesn't preclude God from placing some special calling on your life, a unique job for you to do. But more important than what God might call you to *do* is the kind of person God is calling you to *be*. If you are not becoming the fully mature person God is calling you to be—a person of sustainable faith, hope, and love—you are limiting what you can do in service to Christ.

And so count me as an advocate for a more sustainable discipleship—one that takes seriously Jesus' statement that the yoke is easy and the burden is light.

Sustainable discipleship is not driven by accomplishment, and it is not results-oriented. Instead it focuses on the *process* of growing in Christ, trusting the Holy Spirit to do the work of transformation as we cooperate in the ways that we know how.

In this section, we will walk through the three primary virtues of the Christian life—faith, hope, and love—and discover the process by which a Christian can sustainably live well. My assumption, as you'll see, is that people who practice genuine Christian faith, hope, and love in all of their relationships become the kind of people who introduce healing rather than brokenness into their world. And they find healing for their own brokenness as well.

In other words, they live well.

Chapters 6, 7, and 8 deal with growing faith, hope, and love respectively. Growing in these areas requires more than education or practicing a skill; it requires healing. So each chapter begins with a story from the Gospels in which a broken person finds (or rejects) the healing that is available in Christ's kingdom. But before we get there, we need to focus on the process of growth itself and how our growth in living well can be sustainable. So let's dig in.

Do You Want to Be Healed?

What kind of question is that, right? You may think healing is impossible. You might not believe God is *willing* to put you back together again. But if it's a question of desire, then absolutely you want to be healed, right?

Not so fast; it's a penetrating question, cutting to the heart of all the ways we're broken.

Jesus asked the question to a man who had been lying by a pool for more than thirty-eight years, waiting to be healed. The legend was that occasionally an angel would stir the waters of the pool, and the first person who made it in would be healed (John 5:1–9).

Do you want to be healed?

It seems a silly question. Yet the man didn't give the obvious answer. Instead he began to explain. *It's not my fault. No one will help me get to the pool. Someone always gets there faster.* There were so many good reasons why, after thirty-eight years, he was still lying by the pool waiting for a miracle.

Do you want to be healed?

The answer is obvious only when healing is not really an option. When healing is a genuine possibility, it presents a dilemma, because healing means change. It offers opportunities, removes barriers, introduces new challenges, adds responsibilities, eliminates excuses.

Healing messes with the lifestyle to which we've become accustomed. So often, our desire for healing is undermined by our resistance to change.

Do you want to be healed?

In the first part of this book, I outlined the story of redemption that God is writing in the world. God created humanity and placed us in the perfect environment to thrive. We had the opportunity to experience robust, healthy relationships with God, one another, ourselves, and creation. When the first man and woman rebelled against God, they introduced sin and brokenness into the world. At that moment, God could have destroyed the earth and everything in it and started over again. But he didn't. Rather than react in anger, he responded with mercy and love and began to implement a plan to put back together again everything that was broken—to redeem creation and restore humanity in every way.

He wants you to be part of his story of redemption. He wants you to see that you too are ReCreatable.

At some point in your life, maybe today, Jesus will ask, "Do you want to be healed?"

Understand that the question is not "Do you want to be a Christian?" or "Do you want to have eternal life?" Those are important questions, but this a different question: Do you want Jesus to put your life back together again? Do you want him to fix what's broken within you? Do you want him to heal and restore your relationships with him, others, yourself, and his creation? Do you want to become the person God created you to be in the first place? Do you want to really live well?

Do you want to be healed?

If the answer is yes, then Jesus says, "Get up, take up your bed, and walk."

Learning to Walk

There are no born walkers. Most of us are born with the *potential* to walk, but walking is neither natural nor automatic. In fact, there are several preliminary steps before a newborn baby can even think about walking. She has to develop muscle tone and coordination, then learn to sit up and stand. The first few steps are always an adventure, with the parents helicopering to keep the toddler from danger.

But eventually, the child stops *trying* to walk and just starts walking. No longer does she have to think about how to get from here to there; she just does it, because she has mastered the skill of walking. It didn't come naturally, but now it *feels* natural. Walking has become *second nature*.

Christians are not born walking either; we have to learn to walk before we can run after Jesus. This is not a matter of salvation or conversion; it's about what happens after we're reborn.

Learning to walk in Christ means to let his redemption work through every aspect of your life and relationships, so that your brokenness is being healed and you are being put back together again. It means learning to live well in a way that is sustainable, not one that leaves you feeling overwhelmed and full of guilt. This is what the apostle Paul meant when he said to "work out your own salvation."

Too often, Christians have thought it was simply not possible to be healed in this way, at least not in this life.

But Jesus is sincere when he asks the question, "Do you want to be healed?" And God is serious when he calls you to be holy, because he is holy (1 Pet. 1:16). The expectation was never hypothetical, and the question is not a tease. God expects you to be holy, and he provides the way for you to do it.

The question is, "Do you really want it?"

If you do want to move toward healing in all of your relationships, toward authentic holiness, toward following Jesus as second nature, there is a pathway. It begins with a single step.

Initiative

Some toddlers learn to walk more quickly than others. There are many reasons for this, some of which the toddler has no control over. But there is one thing even toddlers have control over: desire. Some kids just want it more than others. When Jesus healed the man at the pool of Bethesda, he didn't force the man up on his feet and manually put one foot in front of the other for him. He asked the man to take the initiative to stand up and walk.

Sometimes people have mistakenly thought that, once you become a Christian, everything else comes more or less naturally, that it should be easy to do this or that and avoid doing the other.

It just doesn't happen that way. You have to learn to walk.

Many Christians, particularly those who belong to the Reformation tradition (in other words, they are Protestant, not Catholic or Orthodox), stumble over the idea that God actually expects something from us. "Wait," they say, "salvation is by grace alone through faith alone; our righteousness is filthy rags in God's sight." That's all true enough; you're not saved by your good works.

But genuine salvation always leads to a transformed life.

Always.

Jesus says, "I've healed you. Now it's time to get up and walk."

Persistence

Toddlers don't turn into walkers in an instant. They have to learn to shift their weight and keep their balance. That takes time. It's not a skill they're born with, and the only way to pick it up is to begin taking steps.

Learning to walk is a process of trying and failing and learning from your mistakes. John doesn't tell us whether the man at the pool had difficulty walking again after thirty-eight years; perhaps it was like riding a bicycle, and he just "got on again" and went.

When you become a Christian, though, walking with Christ is a brand new skill. After years of brokenness, you don't typically learn to live well in a day. There are starts, stops, and tumbles. You try one thing until you figure out that it doesn't work, and then you try another. Every day you get a bit closer to walking, until suddenly you sense you're starting to get it. And eventually, the patterns of walking in Christ—of living well—become second nature to you. Doing the right thing in a particular area no longer requires intense focus and effort. It flows from who you have become in Christ.

But maybe not today. Today you're learning to walk, and that requires persistence. You know that for now you're going to fall.

You're going to bruise yourself and sometimes others. But learning to walk means getting yourself back up and taking another step.

Discernment

The more a child tries to walk, the more she begins to recognize what makes her fall. Certain movements cause her to lose her balance. Certain obstacles always trip her up. As she begins to discern the things that cause her to fall and figures out how to navigate around them or avoid them entirely, walking becomes more natural for her.

It's the same when you learn to walk the way of holiness. There are obstacles in your walk with Christ. Some of them are entirely avoidable; others are not. Learning to walk means discerning the dangers and figuring out the best way over, under, around, or through them.

So yes, authentic holiness means learning to manage the sin that so easily finds its way into your life. But it's important to go beyond the negative of sin management. Authentic holiness is not the absence of sin; it is being set apart for the service of Christ. Holiness is as much or more about what you do as about what you don't do; more about who you are than who you are not.

Please don't think that because I'm giving just a few paragraphs in this whole book to the topic of managing sin, I consider it an insignificant issue. Far from it.

Let me be clear: Sin is the destroyer of all that you love. It is the reason for the mess that the world is in.

And the thing about sin it that it's not just out there somewhere. As Aleksandr Solzhenitsyn put it, "If only there were evil people somewhere insidiously committing evil deeds, and it were necessary only to separate them from the rest of us and destroy them. But the line dividing good and evil cuts through the heart of every human being. And who is willing to destroy a piece of his own heart?"*

The last thing I want to do is diminish the significance of sin. But the way to eradicate sin from your heart is not to focus on eliminating sin; it is to "put on the Lord Jesus Christ" (Rom. 13:14). And to that task we will soon turn.

Spiritual Muscle Memory

The way to master the skill of walking or any physical challenge is to practice it and develop muscle memory. As you perform the same action repeatedly, your muscles develop a rhythm or pattern. It's as if they begin to memorize that particular motion, so that eventually, they duplicate the motion with little or no conscious thought.

That's why basketball players spend hours at the free throw line, making the same shot over and over again. They are developing muscle memory so that in the big game they can step up to the line and put their body on autopilot. They block out the external and internal noise, and their body takes care of the rest.

Former Yale president and commissioner of Major League Baseball Bart Giamatti put it this way:

> When either athlete or actor can bring all these skills to bear
> and focus them, then he or she will achieve that state of com-
> plete intensity and complete relaxation—complete coherence
> or integrity between what the performer wants to do and
> what the performer has to do. Then, the performer is free;
> for then, all that has been learned, by thousands of hours of

---

*Aleksandr I. Solzhenitsyn, *The Gulag Archipelago*, trans. Thomas P. Whitney (New York: HarperCollins, 1973), 168.

practice and discipline and by repetition of pattern, becomes natural. Then intellect is upgraded to the level of an instinct. The body follows commands that precede thinking.*

The pianist plays her scales every day and the golfer spends hours at the driving range to develop the muscle memory that eventually makes their play look effortless to others. In reality, it took tremendous, repetitive effort in the past to produce the mastery that makes today's performance appear effortless. The muscle memory these people cultivate has resulted in complete coherence between what they want to do and what they have to do.

What if you could develop this kind of spiritual muscle memory in your walk with Christ?

Not only is it possible, it is essential. If you want to be able to do the right thing when the pressure is on, you have to put in the time and discipline to develop Christlike patterns of thought and behavior.

With the help of the Holy Spirit, you can train yourself to think and act in ways that reflect the glory of God. You can develop Christlike thoughts and behaviors so that they become almost natural.

The Power of a Habit

Developing muscle memory is similar to acquiring a new habit. Habits are the things you do automatically without thinking. Your habits are learned; you weren't born with them. But now they are second nature to you; you do them by default.

Your habits are significant because they control your actions,

---

*A. Bartlett Giamatti, *Take Time for Paradise: Americans and Their Games* (New York: Bloomsbury, 2011), 29.

unless you intentionally choose to override them. And when you try to do that, you learn that it requires a lot of effort.

We mostly notice habits when they are destructive and we have to find some way to overcome them. But habits may just as well be good, productive habits. So don't think of habits in a negative way. It's all about what kind of habits you have. Doing the right thing without thinking is a very good place to be.

There are certain things that should never become *merely* habit, such as worship. But it is a good thing simply to show up at worship each weekend without having to decide whether to attend. When you're worshipping, you want your heart and mind engaged, but in a way, it's better if the showing up part becomes automatic. It's good to habitually turn to your Bible or to prayer.

The value of a good habit is that it helps you begin to do the right thing without a lot of effort or willpower.

Automatic Virtue

But what if you could develop habits—spiritual muscle memory—regarding weightier matters than getting up and going to church on Sunday morning? What if you could develop habits of compassion or gentleness or faithfulness, so that these became your automatic response, rather than something you have to convince yourself to do?

This is precisely what Peter meant when he said that Christians should "make every effort to supplement your faith with virtue" (2 Peter 1:5). A virtue is a positive character trait that has become second nature.

You are probably reluctant to think of yourself as virtuous or holy, and with good reason. These are qualities that you should never really feel you have mastered. Still, there is no question that the New Testament says you should strive to live a holy life, and that the way to do this is by developing virtues—patterns of behavior that reflect God's glory.

The church, for a variety of reasons, has often lost touch with the New Testament vision of discipleship and spiritual formation through the patient, disciplined development of Christian virtue.

Yet this is the pathway to becoming the person God created you to be. It is the pathway to healing in all of your relationships. It is the pathway to authentic holiness. The person who is automatically virtuous is the person who lives well.

One caveat before moving on. Spiritual growth requires genuine human effort. It is hard work. This is true. But it does not mean that you can accomplish it or make it happen by your own power or authority. You are saved by grace, a gift of God, and you are sanctified and made holy for his purposes by grace as well.

Yet in both cases, God requires your cooperation. There is nothing you can do to earn God's favor; but you must welcome the gift. And there is nothing you can do to achieve holiness in your own power; but you must work out our salvation. You must put in the effort to develop the habits that lead to godliness. As you do these things, God will grow the Christian virtues in your life through the Holy Spirit.

So, while I will focus in this book mostly on what you must do—on the command to rise and walk—this does nothing to diminish the glory of God and your absolute dependence on him.

Three Battlefields of Virtue

As powerful as habits can be, there are powers, even within you, that conspire to prevent you from developing good habits. There are three battlegrounds for virtue in your life. Winning the battle on one front makes it easier to achieve victory in the other two. Alternatively, if you let your guard down on one front, the other two will often suffer too. The rest of this book is about how you can cooperate with the Holy Spirit, achieve victory on these three battlegrounds, and move closer to a life of authentic holiness.

Thoughts

The way you think has a huge influence on the way you act.

The alarming thing about that is that you are not absolutely, completely in control of the way that you think.

On the one hand, society is constantly feeding you data, images, and ideas. You couldn't put an end to it even if you tried. You're a child of the environment in which you live, and that means others have the freedom to introduce new thoughts into your mind. These enter your mind uninvited, not usually as fully formed thoughts, but as impressions, ideas, images. They can take root there in your mind and begin to influence you, even without your consent or knowledge.

At the same time, you are constantly feeding yourself data, images, and ideas by the choices you make—to read what you read, watch what you watch, go where you go, and do what you do. You may not be aware that you are shaping your mind by the choices you make, but you are. That's why you need to be intentional about guarding your mind.

That is not to say you can—or even should—exclude from your mind every idea or image that is opposed to Christ and the way of holiness. You can learn from both the wise and the foolish. But you do need to exercise discernment, to be aware of how what you read, watch, and think affects you.

Never watch mindlessly or read uncritically. Always filter your thoughts, identify those things that would lead you down the wrong path, and mentally eject them from your system.

Feelings

Your heart, in biblical terminology, is the seat of your emotions. And your emotions can affect your actions as much as or more than your thoughts do.

How often have you known exactly what you needed to do, but you just didn't feel like doing it? And how often have your feelings won that battle?

Or think of it the other way: How often have you you hatched a plan in your mind, but then you just didn't feel right about it? And so your heart—your emotions—prevented you from doing the wrong thing?

Your emotions are not an absolute dictator over your life. When you need to, you can make yourself do the right thing even when you don't feel like it. But your feelings are highly influential.

I'm not arguing that your mind should always trump your heart. Sometimes your heart can lead you to do something other than the wrong thing you had planned to do! Instead, I'm saying that you need to be aware of how your emotions influence your decisions, so that you only let them lead when they direct you down the pathway to authentic holiness.

Behaviors

In the end, following Jesus to become the person he created you to be, living well, is not about how you think or feel but about what you do.

Your mind is flooded with information—thoughts, data, images—some of which you choose for yourself and a lot of which others choose for you. You are not controlled by your thoughts, but neither can you completely control them. The best you can do is bring order to them so that they shape you in the way of Christ rather than leading you down a different pathway.

The same thing is true regarding your emotions. You can't always control the way you feel. The best you can do is to understand your feelings so you can follow them when appropriate and ignore them at other times.

But your will is different. You always do what your will tells you to do.

Part of what it means to be human is that every moment of every day, you have the capacity to choose to do what is right. This means it is a theoretical possibility to make the right decision every day all the time.

There is no biblical reason to say that you must mess up some of your decisions. Now, the reality is that we all do. But that is not a *necessity*. And no good comes from telling yourself that you're bound to mess up, especially when the Bible nowhere teaches that we must sin. It teaches that we do, but not that we must.

The will is the ultimate battleground of holiness, and so we have to filter and shape our thoughts and emotions so that we can act in a way that honors Christ and advances his kingdom.

Some have said that it all starts with your mind. But it can just as easily go in the opposite direction: what you do affects the way you think and feel.

And that's part of the value of Christian habits or virtues. The more you *do* the right thing, the more you shape your thoughts and emotions so that doing the right thing becomes second nature.

Doing It Automatically

In the past few years, I've spent a lot of time with my son Micah teaching him the fundamentals of playing baseball. We spent a lot of time with me on one knee, tossing the ball to Micah. I showed him how to hold his glove up at his chest and his other hand up too, ready to catch the ball with both hands. And I tossed the ball to him hundreds of times, maybe thousands.

At first, it didn't matter how many balls he caught and how many he dropped. It was all about learning the proper technique, so that eventually catching the ball would come naturally. He wouldn't even have to think about it.

When we practiced hitting, I would remind him to place his feet shoulder width, choke up on the bat, hold his hands out away from his body, hold his back elbow up, and point the bat toward the sky. And after several times, I think it was the second day of practicing his hitting, he said, "Look, I'm doing it automatically!"

And that's the point. It's not how many times he hits the ball over my head; it's that he learns to use the right technique so that it becomes natural for him when he steps up to the plate in a real game.

It's the same way with learning to live well. It's all about choosing to act in faith, hope, and love, no matter what you're currently thinking or feeling. And the more you live this way, in the power of the Holy Spirit, the more natural it becomes.

In the next three chapters, I will begin to show how you can develop spiritual muscle memory and learn to walk in the three great Christian virtues of faith, hope, and love. If you want to be healed, you can. It's time to take up your bed and walk!

Personal Reflection

1. What tends to make the Christian life feel unsustainable to you?
2. Do you want to be healed?
3. Do you think it's possible to develop spiritual muscle memory? Is the possibility attractive to you? Why or why not?

4. Which part of developing a good habit is most difficult for you: initiative, persistence, or discernment? Why do you think this is?

5. Which of three battlefields of discipline—thoughts, feelings, or behaviors—are you struggling most with currently? What would change if you were to start experiencing victory on that battlefield?

6. In what area of your walk with Christ would you most like to begin experiencing sustainable growth right away?

Next Steps

1. Acknowledge to God, yourself, and perhaps one other person any guilt or sense of defeat that you're experiencing in your walk with God.

2. Pray that God will begin to give you an understanding of what sustainable discipleship might look like in your life.

3. Begin paying attention this week to whether your actions tend to be more influenced by your thoughts or your emotions. Focus on bringing your thoughts and emotions under the control of your will.

4. Choose one small change to make in your life this week, something that's not too intimidating but is still a positive change. Focus on exercising your will to make the change even when your thoughts or feelings seem to stand in your way.

Chapter 6
FAITH

Faith . . . is the art of holding on to things your reason has once accepted, in spite of your changing moods.

—C. S. Lewis

I believe; help my unbelief!"

It was an honest declaration of imperfect faith. The man believed, but he hadn't mastered his faith yet; he was still learning to walk.

He had come to the right place though. An unclean spirit was wreaking havoc with his son's personality, destroying his life and relationships (Mark 9:14–27). Jesus wasn't available at the moment, but his disciples were. And Jesus had empowered them to heal the sick and cast out demons.

Only in this case, they couldn't.

They had tried, but apparently they weren't masters of their faith yet either. Perhaps it should have been them who cried out, "We believe; help our unbelief!"

The desperate father grew frustrated with the disciples. He argued with them until finally Jesus returned. After explaining the situation, the man said to Jesus, "If you can do anything, have compassion on us and help us."

Jesus replied, "If you can! All things are possible for one who believes."

Those three words, "if you can," caught Jesus' attention. It wasn't because they offended him but because they revealed an opportunity for growth. They moved Jesus to probe deeper into the man's faith.

Help My Unbelief

With the man at the pool of Bethesda, it was a question of desire: "Do you want to be healed?" Here, instead of desire, it was a question of faith: "Do you believe your son can be healed?"

Again, the question was not a backdoor way of asking, "Do you want to be a Christian?" or "Do you want to go to heaven?" Jesus' question was a question of faith applied to the man's deepest concern in life: "Do you believe I can heal your son? Do you believe that I can speak and your son will walk home with you today a new person?" True or false? Yes or no? Do you believe?

Do you believe I can give you new life?

Do you believe I can put your son's life back together again?

Do you believe I can heal your relationship with your mother?

Do you believe I can help you learn to live within your means?

Do you believe I can put your marriage back together again?

Do you believe I can relieve your stress and anxiety?

Do you believe I can help you resolve that situation with your boss?

Do you believe I can give you hope and a purpose?

Do you believe you are a part of my plan to redeem the universe?

Do you believe you can and will do greater things than I have done?

Do you believe?

I believe; help my unbelief!

Jesus may be asking you such a question today. You are reading this book because at some level you want Jesus to put your life back together again. You want him to bring healing to your relationships. You want to experience redemption in some aspect of your life. You want to become the kind of person God created you to be.

You may have already made a declaration of faith in Christ. You may be, like the disciples, trying to walk with Jesus every day and learn at his feet.

But maybe today, when you look at your life, you're like the man who said, "*If you can*, will you please do something."

Or maybe, like the disciples, you're saying, "Wait, I thought you said that I could. Why can't I?"

And here's the thing: Jesus is looking for more than *if you can*. *If you can* translates as, "I need to grow in my faith."

It's not that Jesus requires perfect faith before he changes your life, but he does require *genuine* faith and a desire to grow in that faith. He's holding out for, "I believe; help my unbelief."

Faith and Doubt Can Get Along

That statement, drawn out of the man by Jesus, is an insightful one. It recognizes that truth and doubt often coexist within the same person. A person can truly believe and yet still have room to believe more. A person can have genuine faith and yet still have much room to grow in their faith.

It's like the person who knows a few chords but is still learning to play the guitar. Even for the experienced guitar player, there is always more to be learned and the potential to play better. But you don't have to be a master guitar player before you can make music with a band.

Growing your faith is like learning a new skill, with plenty to learn as you go along. But having even a little faith makes it possible for you to do some pretty great things.

Faith Is a Gift

The man's statement is also remarkable because it shows an awareness of where genuine faith originates from: it is a gift of God.

Yes, we have to exercise our will to believe, but it's God who gives us the capacity to believe, and it's God's faithfulness that gives us a reason to believe. And if we're to grow in our faith, that will be a gift from God as well.

But like the gift of a guitar or any instrument, faith is a useless gift unless we embrace it, make it our own, and learn to use it.

Learning to follow Jesus, becoming authentically holy, comes from developing the habits, the spiritual muscle memory, to follow through on the gift we've been given. Following Jesus becomes second nature as we develop virtues—spiritual habits—like faith.

Relax and Learn to Drive

Before you can legally get behind the wheel of a car, you have to prove you know certain things about driving. But passing the written test does not equal having the ability to drive.

No one is born knowing how to drive, and it cannot be learned from a book. You have to get the feel of handling a car, making left and right turns, making smooth stops, and being aware of what's going on around you at all times. Driving requires practical skill that can only be learned by experience. It's out on the road where you earn the ability to drive.

Beginning drivers are often overwhelmed by all the little things they have to think about and pay attention to in order to safely operate a vehicle. But eventually, with enough experience, you get to a place where you can just relax and drive. Driving becomes second nature to you. Then one day you arrive safely at your destination and realize you don't remember making any of the stops or turns along the way. It's like you were on autopilot. It's a little scary.

Skilled drivers still face challenges that require sharp thinking and quick reflexes. But most often, your good driving habits will carry you to your destination with little conscious effort. And when there is danger, those same habits will be more likely to see you through safely.

Discipleship—learning to follow Jesus—follows a similar pattern. There is a basic amount of head knowledge you need to acquire, but the real learning comes when you put it into practice. You learn not only new ways of thinking but also a new pattern of life that is rooted in faith.

As a new believer, you may feel overwhelmed by all the things, big and small, that require your attention. But with experience, you develop skill in living the Christian life. The new way of thinking and acting becomes second nature, and it no longer requires constant attention or extraordinary effort to stay on the pathway. You can just relax and live a faithful life.

Sure, you still encounter challenges that require your focused attention and quick judgment. But even then, your deeply engrained thoughts and habits help you to react more quickly and decisively to do the right thing.

This is part of what I mean by sustainable faith. Through the power of the Holy Spirit, you can acquire both the basic head knowledge and the practical experience necessary to make following Jesus second nature. Holiness does not come naturally, but it can *become* natural to you.

Three Components of Genuine Faith

The concept of faith is fuzzy in our culture. Some people think of faith as nothing more than a fantasy, an illusion that makes you feel better about your life and where it's going. Others think of faith as contrary to science and reason—that you have to suspend your critical thinking skills in order to embrace it. But neither of these is biblical faith.

If there are three battlegrounds of virtue—our thoughts, feelings, and behaviors—then it should be no surprise that there are three components of genuine faith, each corresponding to one of the battlegrounds.

Belief (Mind)

Faith involves believing that something is true, and this is an activity of the mind. If you are presented with a series of statements that claim to be truth, you either believe them or not. In one sense, the "belief" aspect of faith could be measured by a true-or-false exam. You can determine, for example, whether a person's faith is Muslim, Jewish, Hindu, or Baha'i by giving the person a series of statements and asking the person to judge whether each statement is true or false. The belief aspect of faith involves specific content or propositions, and it means making an intellectual decision to check the "true" box on the exam. Faith is *more* than this kind of intellectual belief, but it is never less.

Trust (Heart)

Faith also involves trust, and this trust is an activity of the heart or emotions. It's one thing to say you believe something is true, but quite another when there's an element of risk involved. Trusting means being willing to risk your life or well-being or that of those you love for the things you claim to believe.

Trust is allowing your beliefs to guide you at life's major and minor turning points. You can't measure this aspect of faith on a true/false exam; this is the practical application part of the exam. For example, you may say that your neighborhood is safe, but do you lock your doors at night? What precautions do you take to protect yourself, your family, your possessions? Faith involves belief, but it goes beyond the intellectual element to matters of trust. And there is more.

Loyalty (Will)

Genuine faith always involves an element of loyalty or faithfulness, and this is an activity of your will. When faith is genuine, it permeates your lifestyle. Others will be able to tell that you believe by how you live and the decisions you make. There is a faithfulness—a consistency—that comes from genuine faith. You won't declare a thing true at one moment when it's convenient to do so and then turn your back on that truth at another moment when it creates a conflict or threat. Genuine faith doesn't waver based on the circumstances or on whether it's convenient or pleasant to believe; it's reflected in every decision that you make and every action that you take.

I believe; help my unbelief.

Right? Every Christian is a mixture of faith and doubt. None of us follows Jesus perfectly. None of us exhibits 100 percent genuine faith at every moment. However, learning to walk in the Christian faith involves training in the power of the Holy Spirit to grow in Christian belief, trust, and faithfulness so that you have more faith this year than you did a year ago. You are living more consistently in June than you were in January. Being a disciple of Jesus becomes second nature as you grow in your belief, trust, and faithfulness.

Six Essential Truths of the Christian Faith

Since faith includes intellectual belief, growing in faith may require becoming more acquainted with the content of the Christian faith. In the first part of this book, we surveyed the content of the Christian faith from the perspective of the story of redemption God is writing in the heavens and earth.

How might we summarize that story, using true/false statements that we can choose to believe or not, to trust or not?

Here's one attempt to do so. There are other ways to summarize the story in a set of doctrinal beliefs, but I believe this set of statements captures the essence of what you need to grasp not only in order to become a Christian but also to make a good start on the pathway of discipleship.

Here are six true/false statements along with some commentary on each. The commentary is designed to show that the six beliefs are based on the story that was outlined in the earlier part of the book.

These are not bare doctrinal statements; they are plot points. But you either believe these statements or you don't. Together, they form a summary of the truest story of the universe and the intellectual foundation for the Christian faith.

1. *The universe has a spiritual dimension.*

"In the beginning, God created the heavens and the earth" (Gen. 1:1). One of the most basic beliefs of Christianity is that there is more to the universe than we can see and touch. There is an invisible, spiritual reality that the author of Genesis called the "heavens," and there is an intelligent Creator whom the author of Genesis called "God." The Bible speaks of heaven or the heavens as the place where the invisible spiritual powers of the universe operate. God is in heaven, along with his holy angels; so are the spiritual forces of evil.

Despite the common misconception, the Bible never pictures heaven as some distant place, far beyond the starry skies. On the contrary, the heavens envelop the earth like its atmosphere. God, the angels, and whatever devils there may be do not operate from "someplace out there"; instead, they are as close as the air that we breathe, if only we could see them.

In fact, the book of Genesis implies that the heavens and the earth were originally even more closely intertwined. When God first created humanity, he walked alongside them in the garden in the cool of the day. But when the first man and woman rebelled and sinned against God, in some mysterious way they initiated a separation between heaven and earth.

Still, the Bible teaches and Christians have always believed that at certain times and places, heaven and earth still intersect, that God still acts within space and time, and that this is not so much supernatural as simply the way things were always supposed to be.

2. History is going somewhere.

History is not a never-ending cycle; instead, there is a "story" aspect to the universe, a drama that is playing itself out in history. Against those philosophies and religions that believe that history is circular or evolutionary, the Christian faith has always argued that human history has a beginning, a middle, and an end. While there may indeed be patterns and cycles in history, there are also characters and a plot and dramatic tension. There is a climax and there will be a final resolution. History is not random or just rambling along; it is going somewhere.

More specifically, history is a true story that is being written by the God who created the universe. He did not create the universe and leave it to run on its own. He is actively involved in guiding events and history to the conclusion that he has already determined.

3. History is about sin, brokenness, and redemption.

The story that God is writing in the universe is one of redemption that powerfully demonstrates the creator God's grace, mercy, and love. It results in God's glory filling the earth as originally intended. God created the earth as the perfect environment for humanity, which was to be the crown of his creation. Our calling as human beings was to reflect God's glory into every corner of his created universe. We were to do this, in part, by living in perfect harmony with God, one another, ourselves, and creation. Instead of embracing this God-given vocation, the first man and woman decided they would prefer to be equal with God, at least in the knowledge of good and evil. By grasping for what did not rightfully belong to them, they introduced sin and rebellion into God's universe, as well as brokenness. Instead of perfect fellowship in every relationship, the history of humanity ever since has been one broken relationship after another.

However, rather than lashing out in anger and destroying the creation which humanity had marred, God set in motion a plan to redeem humanity along with all creation. Toward that end, he called a man named Abraham to be the father of a nation with whom he would make a covenant of redemption. All who embraced the covenant by faith in God could experience forgiveness of their sins, redemption of their lives, and restoration in all their relationships, not to mention eternal life.

4. The pivotal point of history is Jesus' life, death, and resurrection.

Unfortunately, the nation God called seemed to be infected with the same disease as the rest of humanity. Overall, they did not demonstrate faith like Abraham. Eventually, they fell under the judgment of God. They were defeated and sent into exile because of their sin. But God revealed his righteousness—his faithfulness to his covenant with Abraham—by sending Jesus to do what Israel could not do: to faithfully carry out God's plan of redemption for the world.

In his letter to the Ephesians, the apostle Paul said: "In him [Jesus] we have redemption through his blood, the forgiveness of our trespasses, according to the riches of his grace, which he lavished upon us, in all wisdom and insight making known to us the mystery of his will, according to his purpose, which he set forth in Christ as a plan for the fullness of time, to unite all things in him, things in heaven and things on earth." (Eph. 1:7–10)

The centerpiece of human history is the life, death, and resurrection of Jesus of Nazareth. In some way we can't fully understand—though theologians still argue endlessly about it—Jesus once for all brought upon himself all the sin, guilt, and brokenness not only of Israel but of humanity, so that all who bind their lives to his by faith can experience God's grace, mercy, and forgiveness now and for all time. By his death, Jesus provided atonement for sin for all those who believe; and by his resurrection, he provided the opportunity for all those who believe to experience redeemed, restored, eternal life in his kingdom. In Jesus, God is at work putting heaven and earth back together again, redeeming humanity and all creation.

5. You are invited to experience and participate in God's redemption.
To take it one step further, Christian faith teaches that anyone can participate in God's new covenant and kingdom by faith in God through his son, Jesus Christ. Because of Jesus' life, death, and resurrection, you can experience forgiveness of sins. You can be received into his covenant and become a citizen of his kingdom. You can be adopted, in fact, as a child of the King. Even though your life and relationships have been broken by your sin and rebellion, not to

mention the sin of others, you can experience healing and wholeness leading to eternal life.

By faith in Christ, you can experience the redemption of your life. God will work in your heart to bring healing in your relationship with him, with others in your life, with yourself, and with God's creation. You are invited to become part of the story of redemption that God is writing in history. In other words, your story can go somewhere too. You are not stuck in sin, rebellion, and brokenness, doomed to repeat the pattern endlessly. Instead, you have a hope and a future that promises a new kind of life, life as it was always intended to be lived.

6. Redemption only comes through repentance and faith in the Lord Jesus Christ.

The gospel is this: Jesus is Lord and Redeemer. There is no one else who deserves our allegiance, no one else who can offer genuine redemption and restoration. If you want to live well—to embrace authentic humanity—the only way to get there is through Jesus. Placing your faith in Jesus requires repentance and turning away from the attitudes and habits that diminish others and destroy relationships and toward a life of faith, hope, and love.

The Christian faith may be more than the sum of these truths, but it is not less. As you internalize these truths, you are embracing the story that shapes your life as a Christian.

Yes, these truths can be stated as points of doctrine; but the doctrinal points are nothing more than a convenient way to remember and understand the true story. And as you begin to see your life as part of this larger story, your life will be shaped by it, and you will find yourself well on the way to living well.

Six Strategies to Grow in Faith

Once you grasp the basic beliefs of the Christian faith, you may find yourself with the same request as the man who brought his son to Jesus to be healed: "I believe; help my unbelief." This is natural and normal. You don't become a hero of faith in a day. Abraham, who in many ways was the father of our faith, spent twenty-five years learning to trust and follow God before his faith was put to the ultimate test.

It is possible, however, to waste the time God gives you to grow your faith, so that you're totally unprepared when a time of testing comes. How can you grow and strengthen your faith? How can following Jesus in faith become second nature so that when the time comes, you can respond in faith without even thinking about it?

Once you've embraced the true story represented in the six truths we've just discussed, growing and strengthening your faith is about working out those truths in every aspect of your mind, heart, and will—that is, in your thoughts, emotions, and behaviors.

As an example, let's look now at the first of these truths—that the universe has a spiritual dimension—and see what practical steps you can take to work out this aspect of your faith. The practices here will be applicable to all of the truths of the Christian faith and help you develop the muscle memory necessary to follow Jesus in faith.

1. Pray for awareness.

Faith is a gift of the Holy Spirit. Developing and growing it requires your cooperation with the Holy Spirit, but you can't do it apart from his work in your life. So if you want to grow in your faith that the universe has a spiritual dimension, begin by praying every day for a certain period—maybe two weeks or a month—that God will bring to you an awareness of the reality of the spiritual aspect of our existence.

During the time that you're praying to be more aware of this particular truth, cooperate with the Holy Spirit. Be intentional about looking for ways that heaven intersects with your daily existence on earth. Note carefully the times and places where you or someone you trust experienced something that seemed to transcend what you can see or touch. Only God can reveal the spiritual dimension of reality to you, but he does so as you actively seek it.

2. Establish memorials.

When God grants you awareness or understanding of a particular truth about the unseen aspects of our universe, find a way to memorialize the truth that God revealed to you, so that you'll remember it later and be able to pass it on to others. This could be as simple as writing down the story, telling it to others in a memorable fashion, or posting a picture online with a descriptive caption. Or it could be expressed creatively through art, poetry, or music.

The purpose of the memorial is not to inspire a great piece of art, although that can certainly happen. It is simply to put down a marker indicating that God spoke to you in this moment and at this place. This is why you'll find several stories in the Old Testament where people such as Abraham, Isaac, and Jacob built altars after a memorable encounter with God. Not only did the altar serve as a place of worship, but it was also a perpetual reminder of the truth that God revealed.

3. Discuss it with other believers.

One of the best ways to reinforce your faith as you grow is to talk about it with others who are also growing in their faith. Make it a point to discuss how you're growing in the faith with at least a couple of other people on a regular basis. Talking about what you're learning cements the truth in your mind. You'll also have the privilege of helping to strengthen others in their faith as you share how you're growing or even how you're struggling. Be sure that you take time to listen too, because you will benefit from the perspectives of other believers, who might see things that you've missed or understand them differently.

As you begin to notice ways that heaven and earth are intersecting in your life, talking about them helps you to acknowledge their reality. Talking about spiritual realities with otherwise normal people in sane tones helps to remove spirituality from the realm of the spooky in your mind and moves it into the realm of belief and genuine faith. By talking openly with other believers about your growing awareness of the spiritual realities beyond our material world, you can also help check one another's experiences against Scripture to be sure that you are interpreting spiritual reality correctly.

4. Note obstacles or objections.

As you grow in the faith, you'll certainly encounter obstacles and objections to faith. Growing in faith doesn't mean that you'll never wrestle with doubt and faith. If anything, the wrestling and doubt can be more intense when your faith is being stretched. The way to grow through times of doubt is not to act as though everything is fine and to sweep the doubts under the rug. It's to acknowledge and address the obstacles and objections as you meet them. By taking each doubt and objection seriously, even if you don't immediately arrive at a satisfying resolution, you'll be growing a faith that can weather even bigger storms later on.

One of the biggest obstacles to belief in the unseen realities of the universe is our modern culture's materialistic mind-set. By materialistic, I don't mean our desire for more things, although that's a *result* of a materialistic mind-set. Instead I mean the fact that our culture is biased against anything that we can't see, touch, or fully explain. The prevailing mind-set is that life is nothing more than atoms and molecules and subatomic particles; that there is nothing outside or beyond the material that breathes life into it or that orders and guides it. So to embrace the biblical truth that there is an unseen, spiritual element to the universe is to go against the major current of our culture.

5. Deepen your understanding.

In this chapter, I have given you six basic truths that are one way of summarizing the Christian faith. These truths are simple enough that you can teach them to your children and new believers, and they can understand them. I hope that you'll do that. But these are also deep truths. In other words, each one deserves a lifetime of study and reflection in itself. You'll never learn everything there is to be learned about even one of these truths. You'll never put them into practice fully and completely before Jesus returns. I don't say this to discourage you; I say it to encourage you to understand that embracing these six truths does not mean that you've mastered belief and the Christian faith. They're only a beginning.

Each of these six truths could inspire ten thousand PhD dissertations. Each could form the basis for a limitless number of works of art, music, and poetry. We could discuss them over coffee every Thursday night for the next twenty-five years and still have something important and significant to discuss. They are entry points to the Christian faith. They are sufficient to lead one to faith in Jesus Christ, but they are also capable guides to help a person grow in faith over the course of a lifetime.

6. Take it with you.

Faith is not genuine unless it begins to permeate your life. Do not confine your faith to Sunday morning worship and small group meetings. Endeavor to live it out on a daily basis. Living it out means to let it soak into every pore of your life, shaping your thoughts, emotions, and behaviors. Let it shape the person you're becoming.

We'll talk more in the third section of this book about the means God provides for the Christian faith to shape your entire life.

Personal Reflection

1. In what ways do you tend to wrestle with intellectual belief in the gospel?
2. In what kinds of situations do you find it difficult to trust in the truth of the gospel?
3. How might your lifestyle need to better reflect your faith in the gospel?
4. Of the six essential truths of the Christian faith, which do you have the hardest time understanding or believing? Why?
5. What are some of the key ways you would like to see yourself grow in faith?
6. How might your life look different—how might you live better—if you were to grow in those ways?

Next Steps

1. Choose one aspect of the Christian faith that you would like to know more about. Then connect with someone you respect—perhaps a pastor, teacher, or other mature Christian in your life—and ask the person to share his or her thoughts on the topic and tell you how you might learn more.

2. Select one of the six essential truths of the Christian faith, one that you believe but wrestle with trusting in it. After reviewing the "Six Strategies" section, create a plan for growing in trust over the next week or month.

3. Spend some time thinking about the last time you experienced a faith crisis. What kinds of things were you thinking, feeling, and doing at the time? Try to determine whether it was a crisis of belief, trust, or loyalty.

4. Now think through what you will do the next time you experience a crisis of faith. How can the perspectives gained in this chapter help you turn that crisis into an opportunity for growing your faith?

Chapter 7

HOPE

What infuses hope with its emotional vigor is the value and
excitement we attach to our beliefs and expectations.
—Matthew Elliott

Rabbi, let me recover my sight."

If you were the blind man at Jericho, how would you have answered Jesus' question: "What do you want me to do for you?" (Mark 10:51; for complete context, read vv. 35–52).

When Jesus asked James and John the same question, they had a ready answer. According to Mark, it happened just before they encountered the blind man. They approached Jesus with a request: "Teacher, we want you to do for us whatever we ask of you."

That's pretty bold, but Jesus didn't flinch. "What do you want me to do for you?" Same question he would ask the blind man.

But the disciples had a different kind of response: "Grant us to sit, one at your right hand and one at your left, in your glory."

And that's a fail.

Later, as Jesus and his disciples were leaving Jericho, Bartimaeus, a blind beggar, started crying out, "Jesus, Son of David, have mercy on me!"

The people around him quickly became annoyed and told him to be quiet. But he didn't; instead, "he cried out all the more."

Finally, Jesus sent someone to bring the blind man to him. When he arrived, Jesus asked the same question he had just asked his disciples: "What do you want me to do for you?"

It's a pregnant question, full of opportunity and hope. How would you have answered it?

Clearly, not any answer would have done; just look at James and John. But Jesus was greatly pleased with Bartimaeus's response.

Rabbi, let me recover my sight.

While Mark doesn't use the word *hope*—in fact, the word *hope* is hardly used in the gospels at all—Bartimaeus demonstrated genuine hope in his encounter with Jesus.

He somehow knew what Jesus wanted to do for him, he believed that Jesus could and would do it, and then he acted in such a way to obtain what was available to him.

After the last chapter, we can easily see that Bartimaeus's answer reflected faith in Jesus. But we should also see that his request was just as full of another key virtue: hope.

According to the apostle Paul, hope is one of the three great Christian virtues (1 Cor. 13:13). Yet while most Christians understand their need to grow in faith and love, many of us rarely think of the significance of hope or how we can grow authentic hope in our lives.

Three Ways to Hope in God

Hope is more than a wish, desire, dream, or goal. We cannot conjure up hope from within. Like faith, genuine hope is a gift from God.

Christian hope is built on God's promises. God made a covenant with his people, and he has proven faithful to his promises. Because he has done precisely what he said he would do, we can know that he will keep the rest of his promises too.

Yet we must own those promises, and the way we claim God's promises is through hope.

By now, you will not be surprised to learn that genuine hope involves all three aspects of human personality: thought, feeling, and behavior.

Vision (Mind)

In one sense, sight or vision is a good metaphor for hope. Hope means grasping or seeing in your mind what God has planned for the universe and for your life so that it becomes real to you.

Vision is a powerful motivator. Organizations invest in identifying and communicating their vision, because vision inspires hope. When people can envision what is possible in the future, not only do they tend to stick around through the difficult times, but they also know better how to help the organization make its vision a reality.

But here's the key: Christian hope is not about creating a vision for your future; it's about discovering the future God has already envisioned for you.

Part of growing in hope is learning to think correctly about the future: not only what will happen when Jesus returns, but what can happen in your life before he returns. So there is a *content* aspect to Christian hope. God has made specific promises regarding the world and his people. To grow in hope, you have to engage your mind, to attempt to grasp the heights of God's plan for you.

Expectation (Heart)

Grasping God's vision for you and the world is part of genuine hope; but it's possible to have intellectual understanding and still reject the hope God offers.

Genuine Christian hope also engages the heart. It moves beyond the knowledge of God's promises to an assurance that God will keep those promises. Just as genuine faith goes beyond belief to trust, genuine hope moves beyond vision to expectation. It is one thing to see the Bible's vision of the future. It is quite another to expect it to happen in just that way.

The St. Louis Cardinals have a rich tradition of winning consistently. They have more world championships (eleven) than any other National League team, and they are consistently in the hunt for a pennant most Septembers. Because of past success, Cardinal fans do not merely wish each spring for a trip to the World Series—we demand it. We know what October is like when our team is in the playoffs and when it is not. We know what it feels like for our team to win the World Series, and we want more of it. For Cardinal fans, this is more than a wish or a dream; it is an expectation. Still, eighty-nine of the last one hundred seasons have ultimately ended in disappointment for Cardinal fans. And even though that 11 percent success rate is the best in the National League, it still reflects a lot of disappointment.

But the hope you have in Christ will not disappoint you. God is faithful. He is true to his word. What he says, he will do. It may feel like a risk to place your hope in God, but it is not. Your hope will be fulfilled in more and better ways than you can possibly imagine.

Anticipation (Will)

But there is more to genuine hope than vision and expectation; those who have genuine hope always begin to anticipate the future.

Sometimes people use the word *anticipation* to mean the same as *expectation*. But the word has another meaning that is something like "acting ahead of time." Anticipating a punch is more than knowing it's coming; it's moving your face out of the way. Anticipating a stock market rebound is more than observing the trend; it's managing your portfolio to take advantage of the potential windfall. If you fail to anticipate a future event, whether the event is good or bad, you have failed to prepare yourself for it. Anticipation means to engage your will—to change your behavior—so that you are prepared for the envisioned future.

Genuine hope moves beyond vision and expectation to anticipation. It goes beyond your mind and heart to actually doing something about it. If it hasn't changed the way you live, then it's not genuine hope. Hope reveals itself through your behaviors.

Learning to hope in Christ is more than just understanding God's promises and expecting their fulfillment; it is ordering your life so that you can fully participate in the new reality that God is creating. And, as we will see, it also means behaving in small ways that can help bring about the kingdom in the part of the world where you live.

Learning to follow Jesus as second nature—living well—means to embrace the hope of Jesus Christ and let it circulate through your veins, so that the hope is always before you and shaping your life at every moment.

Eight Promises to Build Your Hope On

Now that we have this three-part definition of hope—as vision, expectation, and anticipation—we can begin to explore some of the specific promises that make up the Christian hope. These promises fall into two different time frames: *when* Jesus returns and *until* Jesus returns.

This way of dividing up the future assumes one of the primary aspects of the biblical hope: *that* Jesus will return. We'll say more about that in a moment. But for now, understand that Jesus' return will be the second major turning point in human history, with the first being his life, death, and resurrection. We'll start by looking at the distant future: what the Bible says will happen when Jesus returns. Then we'll look at the hope that we have for today and until Jesus returns.

When Jesus Returns

The Bible is clear in its teaching that history is going somewhere, moving toward a final climax. The event that signals that climax will be the return of Jesus. There are many different schemes that attempt to show the events of the "end times," the time of history's climax, in specific detail. It is not my intention to comment in this book on any of those schemes, either to affirm or discredit them. Instead, I want to clearly lay out the key biblical promises regarding what will happen when Jesus returns.

Resurrection

Christians inherit a framework for our future hope from the ancient Jewish faith. By the time Jesus arrived, the Jewish belief was that there would be two major stages of human history: the present age and the age to come, the age of the Messiah. Most of the faithful believed that, when the Messiah came, there would be a resurrection of all the covenant keepers.

What they did not expect was the death and resurrection of the Messiah himself, or his return to heaven, or a period of waiting before the faithful would be raised. Huge surprise.

The apostles were left scrambling to explain why the Messiah died and rose again and why his "inauguration period" was lengthened before the general resurrection (Acts 3:19–21). Paul explained that Jesus' resurrection represented the "firstfruits" of all who would believe (1 Cor. 15:20) and showed that the power of God was with him (Rom. 1:4). He argued that God was delaying the general resurrection to give all people everywhere the opportunity to repent (Acts 17:30–31; Romans 2:4).

The Christian hope is that what God did for Jesus, he will one day do for us too. The resurrection means much more than that, but it does not mean less than that.

Because Jesus of Nazareth died and was raised to life, although we too will die, we can be certain that we will one day be raised again if we remain in Christ.

New Creation

Jesus' resurrection points the way toward another significant part of the Christian hope. When God created heaven and earth, he pronounced everything he created, including humanity, to be "very good." Even though human beings have corrupted God's creation by our sin and rebellion, it's still the habitat best suited for us. God created humanity to live on earth.

God has proven by his patience that he has no interest in destroying his "very good" creation. Wouldn't it be odd if, after several thousand years, God suddenly decided to take us from the only home we've ever known to a place, heaven, which was created for a different purpose?

No. Any time we spend in heaven will only be temporary. God has something better in mind.

Scripture teaches that there will be "a new heaven and a new earth" (Rev. 21:1). Just the fact that there will be a new earth points to its being our eternal home. Humanity was created to inhabit and rule over the earth. When we die, we may have a brief layover in heaven, but our ultimate destiny is eternal life on a new earth that is free from the corruption of sin.

One way of interpreting "a new heaven and a new earth" is that God will destroy the earth and start over again. Another is that he will redeem and restore his creation to pristine condition. This seems to me more likely and consistent with God's character. There is much more that we could say or imagine about the new creation, but this should be enough to inspire a sense of genuine hope.

Judgment

If we are to give an accurate picture of the Christian's future hope, we cannot neglect to talk about the coming judgment. It might seem strange to talk about this under the heading of "hope," yet what kind of future would it be if there were no accounting for all the evil that has been perpetrated over the centuries? While we might not seek judgment for ourselves and those we love, our hearts cry out for there to be an end to the injustice and for sin and evil to be repaid with justice.

Rest assured that the Bible teaches a future judgment. It is not the purpose of this book to speculate on what that will look like or how it will happen or even who will be punished and who will not. I just want to make three key points about justice: (1) when all is said and done, everyone will be able to say that God acted justly in his judgment; (2) everyone will be able to say that God exercised way more mercy than any of us had a right to expect; and (3) everyone will be able to say that those who were faithful to God's covenant were treated exceptionally well by the just Judge.

Glory

When God created heaven and earth, the two were married, linked together in a way that we can only imagine today. As we've mentioned before, God walked in the garden with Adam and Eve, and no one thought it the least bit odd. It was just the way things naturally were. Man and woman lived in perfect harmony with God, one another, themselves, and all of God's creation. God gave man and woman the privilege and responsibility of reflecting his glory into every corner of creation.

When Jesus returns, heaven and earth will be reunited under the gentle and powerful rule of King Jesus (Eph. 1:10). There will no longer be a gulf created by sin separating heaven and earth; instead, "the dwelling place of God is with man. He will dwell with them, and they will be his people, and God himself will be with them as their God" (Rev. 21:3). The New Jerusalem will not need a source of light such as the sun, because "the glory of God gives it light, and its lamp is the Lamb" (Rev. 21:23).

At that time, humanity will finally take up its true calling to reflect the glory of God into every corner of creation, and "the earth will be filled with the knowledge of the glory of the Lord as the waters cover the sea" (Hab. 2:14). And all of those who were faithful to God's covenant will enjoy God's eternal kingdom on the renewed earth for longer than you can possibly imagine.

There is much more to be said about the Christian hope, but this is enough to get you going in the right direction. This is an area that will more than repay the Christian's investment of the time necessary to study and grow in Christian hope.

Until Jesus Returns

Our future hope carries implications for the way we live today. If you have genuine hope in the coming resurrection, new creation, judgment, and glory, then you will begin to *anticipate* the life of the future kingdom here and now. This is part of what Jesus meant when he went around Galilee proclaiming, "The kingdom of God is at hand." He didn't mean that the end of the world was near and everyone would soon be going to heaven or hell; he meant that the kingdom would soon be inaugurated and people would be empowered to live, in many ways, as if his kingdom were already here. And we are to work out what this means in the place where we do life.

A New Creation

If you are part of God's covenant by faith, you are already a new creation. You don't have to wait until Jesus returns for your mind, heart, and will to be transformed or for your broken relationships to be healed. As a believer in Christ, you already have the capability, in the power of the Holy Spirit, to walk the pathway of holiness.

At Sinai, God gave Moses and the people of Israel his Law, his covenant. It defined what it meant to be the people of God and how they were to behave. Overall, they had a tough time with that.

Later, through the prophets, God promised that one day he would write the Law on the hearts of his people. In other words, they would not be burdened by a long list of legal regulations; instead, holiness would be the result of a transformed heart, a renewed Spirit.

That's what I'm saying: if you follow Christ, you have the Law written on your heart.

That doesn't mean you immediately and automatically live by the virtues of faith, hope, and love. But through God's redemption, you are capable of making those virtues a reality in your life.

Because you are a new creation in Christ, you can have genuine victory over the sin and rebellion in your life. Its stranglehold over you has been broken. You don't have to sin or rebel against God anymore.

You may have deeply engrained habits that bend your heart and behaviors away from God. But when you come to Christ, he gives you the power to overcome the sin habits in your life so that they are no longer even natural for you.

Restored Relationships

As you begin to put your sin habits behind you and replace them with habits that flow from Christian faith, hope, and love, you will begin to see that God is bringing healing in your relationships.

As you experience God's grace and mercy, you begin to see him less as a demanding tyrant and more as a loving Father who has adopted you into his family.

As you begin to reshape your thoughts, emotions, and behaviors so that they flow from genuine faith, hope, and love, you will become less self-centered in your relationships and more likely to notice and pay attention to others' needs.

As you begin to see yourself as part of the story of redemption that God is writing in the world, you will became less anxious about life and more at peace with yourself.

As you begin to recognize everything you see, hear, taste, smell, and touch as one of God's good gifts, you are less likely to abuse the gifts and more likely to find yourself at home in the place where you live.

In many cases, it's not that you'll have to "work on your relationships"; it's more that God's redemption will seep into every pore of your body and soul, and your relationships will begin to take care of themselves.

Of course, every relationship has two sides, and not every relationship may be redeemable this side of eternity. But you will be amazed what God can and will do to heal your relationships as you develop the virtues of faith, hope, and love.

Pockets of the Kingdom

I have referred before to "pockets of the kingdom." Wherever Christians come together, in groups of as few as two or three, there you will find God's kingdom at work.

What this means is that when followers of Christ are genuinely behaving toward one another in ways that flow from the Christian virtues of faith, hope, and love, we can experience here and now a small glimpse of what God's eternal kingdom will be like.

It's imperfect. It's not yet complete, because all of us are still in the process of being redeemed and made holy. But it is real.

And when Christians join together in communities that practice faith, hope, and love in all of their relationships, the result is exceptionally attractive to those close enough to observe it. This is "attractional" church at its best.

Part of our calling as a church is to create these pockets of God's kingdom, where faith, hope, and love are written on our hearts and flowing through our behaviors. And the key point I want to communicate right here is that *it can happen in your life right away.* You can experience the kingdom of God here and now. This is part of your present hope.

The Holy Spirit

Always remember that none of this can be accomplished alone. Left to ourselves, we do not develop the virtues of faith, hope, and love. We are still bound to our sinful habits and behaviors. Left alone, we break our relationships and find ourselves clueless as to how to put them back together.

But the great truth is that even though Jesus returned to the invisible, spiritual dimension of reality, he is still with us in the form of his Holy Spirit. And believers in Christ have the promise of the Holy Spirit to stretch, shape, convict, guide, and mold us. This is not the place to go into a full theological definition of the Holy Spirit, but a major part of our present Christian hope is that the Holy Spirit is present and active in our lives, helping us to anticipate and live out our future hope.

Here and now.

Paul said that we can view the Holy Spirit as a down payment on our future inheritance in God's kingdom (2 Cor. 5:5). What you will only *fully* experience in God's eternal kingdom, you can *genuinely* experience now through the presence and power of God's Holy Spirit.

There is so much more that could be said, but again, hopefully I've said enough to get you started in thinking about how God's future hope can be anticipated in your life here and now.

Three Strategies for Cultivating Hope

Jesus prayed the ultimate prayer of hope when his disciples asked him to teach them to pray: "Your kingdom come, your will be done, on earth as it is in heaven" (Matt. 6:10).

This is not a prayer for us to be rescued from hell and spend eternity in heaven. It's a prayer that heaven and all that it entails would come to earth.

Your kingdom come *on earth*.

Your will be done *on earth*.

Jesus was teaching his disciples to pray in hope.

From much of what I've already written, it should be clear how we can grow in Christian hope. We do so by seeking to understand it more fully, by learning to expect that God will do what he promises to do, and finally, by anticipating the coming of his kingdom through our behaviors.

Those three steps—vision, expectation, and anticipation—form a continuous spiral that you can trace deeper into Christian hope (or higher, depending on how you think of it), as deep as you have the time and energy to pursue it in this life. The more you pursue Christian hope, the more your life will reflect God's glory and the better you will be prepared for when Jesus returns to fulfill his promises.

Beyond vision, expectation, and anticipation, a couple of other practices can also further your growth in Christian hope. Let's look at them now.

Seek the Fruit of the Spirit

The apostle Paul identified a number of characteristics that show that the Spirit is transforming us: "love, joy, peace, patience, kindness, goodness, faithfulness, gentleness, self-control"; and also, "those who belong to Christ Jesus have crucified the flesh with its passions and desires" (Gal. 5:22–24).

The more you see the fruit of the Spirit in your life, the more confidence you'll have that God is doing a work in you. And as you see God being faithful to his promises to you, it will strengthen your hope that he will be faithful to all of his promises.

The fruit of the Spirit cannot be conjured up or manufactured in the Christian's life; they are a direct result of the Holy Spirit's work. But while you may not be able to make yourself joyful, for example, you can cooperate with the Holy Spirit by learning to think, act, and behave in the way that joyful people do. As you do, the Holy Spirit will begin to create within you the habit of genuine joyfulness so that it becomes second nature.

Not that it's impossible to develop some of these characteristics—self-control, for example—apart from a relationship with Christ and the power of the Holy Spirit. But the fruit of the Spirit are inclusive. When the Holy Spirit is at work in your life, you'll experience growth in every one of the ways Paul mentions.

Not perfectly. And not overnight. But over time, it will be unmistakable.

And when you begin to see signs of such growth in your life, it will strengthen your hope that there is more to come.

Seek Restored Relationships

Perhaps nothing will strengthen your hope like seeing God begin to transform some of your relationships.

There is a direct connection between the fruit of the Spirit and the transformation of relationships. Imagine what a difference it can make when your interactions with a difficult person are full of genuine love, joy, peace, patience, kindness, goodness, faithfulness, gentleness, and self-control.

Again, not perfectly. But every little bit helps.

Seeking restored relationships, then, is mostly about letting the fruit of the Spirit set the tone for your interactions with others. Of course, relationships have two directions. And just because you change your attitude and approach doesn't guarantee that the other person will. But as you begin to seek restoration and reconciliation in your worn or broken relationships, you will find that the Holy Spirit begins to restore some of them.

In the same way, as you bring the fruit of the Spirit to relationships that were already good, they will grow even stronger.

Watch God work through the changes he is making in your life to restore actual relationships with real people, and you will gain confidence and hope that God has much more in store for you in the future.

Seek Pockets of the Kingdom

Perhaps nothing will help you more as you seek to grow in hope than to find and participate in a pocket of the kingdom where believers are actively seeking to follow Jesus and live out the virtues of faith, hope, and love, as well as the fruit of the Spirit, at every moment.

As you participate in such a community, you will see that God is not only working in your life to transform you but also working in others' lives to transform them. Those people will strengthen your hope and you will strengthen theirs. Much more on this in the final section of this book.

How Blessed We Are

In Paul's great prayer for the Ephesian church (Eph. 1:15–23), he offered thanks to God because he had heard excellent reports of their faith and love. Then he wrote, "I do not cease to give thanks for you, remembering you in my prayers, that the God of our Lord Jesus Christ, the Father of glory, may give you the spirit of wisdom and of revelation in the knowledge of him, having the eyes of your hearts enlightened, that you may know what is the hope to which he has called you, [and] what are the riches of his glorious inheritance in the saints."

Paul said, in effect, "I'm not concerned about your faith or love. You're doing well there. I pray that you would grow in *hope*."

Paul didn't pray that God would bless the church. Instead, he prayed that God would give them the insight to understand how blessed they already were. He prayed for wisdom and revelation so that they could somehow grasp the blessings they'd already received.

That is my prayer for you today. As Jesus opened the eyes of the blind man, Bartimaeus, so may God open the eyes of your heart so you can see and embrace the hope to which he has called you. God has more in store for you than you could ever ask or imagine.

Personal Reflection

1. Who in your life would you describe as genuinely hopeful?
2. What is it like to be around people who are characterized by hope?
3. What is the difference between optimism and biblical hope?
4. What things make it difficult for you personally to have hope?
5. Which of the eight promises mentioned in this chapter fill you with the most hope? Why?

6. What are some ways God has been faithful to you or people you love that give you genuine hope for the future?

Next Steps

1. Take an honest inventory of the fruit of the Spirit in your life. Which ones do you feel are evident? Which might be lacking? Determine to seek the missing fruit in your life and cooperate with the Holy Spirit to facilitate its growth.

2. Review the four promises for *after* Jesus returns. Choose one that interests you and then do a survey of everything you can find in Scripture regarding this hope.

3. Review the four promises for *until* Jesus returns. Choose one that you think could make a big difference in your life right now. Talk with a trusted friend or mentor about your desire to see that aspect of hope begin to permeate and transform your life.

4. Find a creative way—whether through writing, music, art, poetry, or whatever creative means you prefer—to express the hope you have in Christ. Share it with at least one other person as a concrete expression of your Christian hope.

Chapter 8
LOVE

The Christianly virtuous person is not thinking about his or her own moral performance. He or she is thinking of Jesus Christ, and of how best to love the person next door.
—N. T. Wright

What shall I do to inherit eternal life?" (Luke 10:25).

It was a common question. Those who studied the Law loved to debate about the requirements for entering the "age to come," just as many theology students today love to debate about freedom of the will or whether Jesus could have sinned.

There were standard answers too. The answer you gave allowed your discussion partner to quickly place you on the theological grid. To put you in a box.

The man questioning Jesus was far from a novice; he was an expert in the Jewish Law. You'd probably have seen him hanging out on weekends at Jewish cafes, arguing over the finer points of the Law with whoever would give him a minute.

So this man wasn't planning to learn something *from* Jesus. Not really. He was planning to learn something *about* Jesus.

Maybe the man was trying to trip Jesus up—to get him to say something ludicrous to discredit himself.

Maybe he was having auditions for his debating club.

Or maybe he just couldn't resist a good discussion.

What shall I do to inherit eternal life?

Jesus didn't offer one of the standard answers. Instead, he lobbed the question back to the lawyer: "What is written in the Law? How do you read it?" (Luke 10:26).

OK. Fair enough. The lawyer was willing to play it that way. He had his own standard answer, based on Deuteronomy 6 and Leviticus 19, and he didn't mind sharing it.

"You shall love the Lord your God with all your heart and with all your soul and with all your strength and with all your mind, and your neighbor as yourself" (Luke 10:27).

Now, just as with the man at the pool of Bethesda, and just as with blind Bartimaeus, we have to remember that the man's question had not been, "How do I get saved?" or "How do I become a Christian?" or "How can I go to heaven?" as important as those questions are.

The man's question had been, "What shall I do to inherit eternal life?"

This was an insider's question. It was about God's kingdom coming on earth as it is in heaven.

The lawyer wasn't looking for salvation; he was already part of God's covenant people. He would have already considered himself "saved," had they used that distinctly evangelical Christian terminology in his day.

His question wasn't about salvation. Salvation is about faith—always has been, always will be. His question was about sanctification, or more precisely, glorification (Rom. 8:30). It was about preparing for the arrival of the Messiah. It was about authentic holiness, true spirituality, walking with God, living well.

In other words, it was precisely the question we have been asking and attempting to answer here. And the man's answer?

Love God. Love your neighbor.

Jesus' response is not what you might expect: "You have answered correctly; do this, and you will live" (Luke 10:28).

Wow.

If you've ever attended a Christian theology class, you know that is *not* the right answer.

Why didn't Jesus tell the man there was *nothing* he could do to inherit eternal life—that it had all been done for him (or soon would be)? Why didn't he emphasize the need to be sorrowful for his sins and repent of them? What about believing all the correct doctrines?

Why didn't Jesus say, Yeah, love God and love your neighbor—but you *can't do it!* Not well enough, anyway. That's why you need my sacrifice to pay for your sins.

Jesus' real answer just seems so . . . inadequate compared to our more theologically astute answers.

Jesus messes with our theology. And we shouldn't be too quick to try to tidy it up.

Love God. Love your neighbor. If you do, you will inherit eternal life.

Full stop.

And so we come to the heart of what it means to live well. And we're given two commands. Two things we must do. Two things we must not leave undone if we want to continue on the pathway we've started toward eternal life.

This, after all, is why we need faith and hope in the first place. This is their purpose: to provide the foundation we need to love God and our neighbor.

Maybe this is why the apostle Paul said that even though faith and hope will still be with us in the coming age, nevertheless in Christ's kingdom, the greatest, most important thing would be love (1 Cor. 13:13). Love for God and love for others.

That's life in the kingdom, and that's why we need to spend our days here learning to love.

So, now it's time to ask the Lou Gramm question: Do you want to know what love is?

Three Components of Christlike Love

The first time I told my wife Debbie I loved her, more than twenty years ago now, we were sitting in a gazebo on the campus of Welch College in Nashville, Tennessee. It was our sophomore year of college.

She laughed.

Maybe it was for joy (as she now says).

Maybe it was that I stumbled and fumbled around with my words until they actually fought their way out of my mouth (as I remember it).

Or maybe it was because she knew that I couldn't possibly understand what I was saying.

Love is much easier to say than to do. You can't manufacture it or produce it by direct effort; you can only cultivate it in the soil of everyday living and relating.

In other words, you don't marry for love. Not really. You marry for the *potential* of love.

Marital love is a lifetime learning experience. And some of the best reasons to love are only learned after many years of loving.

It's not much different when it comes to learning to love God and others. Let's not be too quick to claim love for God or the masses. There's a good chance we're only beginning to understand what love means.

We should all be crooning with Lou Gramm, "I want to know what love is!" although hopefully with much more noble purposes.

Admittedly, all of this is a far cry from the way love is described, defined, and portrayed in today's society. Our modern definition of love is shaped by the Romantic movement of the eighteenth century and the Existential movement of the nineteenth century.

The Romantic movement gave us love as *pure emotion.*

The Existential movement gave us love as *authentic passion.*

While perhaps there is some truth in each of these definitions, neither of them verges on adequate. Yet these definitions of love dominate in popular movies and TV shows where "love affairs" are sudden, irresistible, passionate, and for the most part, brief and temporary.

Genuine love is something else entirely.

You will not be surprised that it has something to do with your mind, heart, and will.

Respect (Mind)

Love may be a choice, but it's not exactly an unmerited gift. If you want to test that hypothesis, try telling someone you love, "There is absolutely nothing I see in you to love, but—I can't explain it—I love you anyway."

See how well that goes over. (I'm kidding, of course. Please don't!)

Genuine love—we intuitively know this—is based on knowledge. We love because we see characteristics or qualities in another person that make him or her lovable and worthy of respect.

Love engages the mind, and the more you think about what is lovely and respectable in another person the more you will love her or him. Those who love well make it a practice to meditate on the qualities they see in other people which make them worthy of love and respect. And by the way, as Christians, we ought to be able to see and appreciate the attractiveness of other people without being consumed by a desire to have them or a lust to possess them.

When love is based on knowledge, we think carefully about the best way to act on our love rather than simply doing what might come easily or naturally. Love is not doing the first thing that comes to mind to express our feelings; it involves carefully considering what is in the other person's best interests. This is why some ways of expressing affection are best kept within marriage. It's also why some ill-conceived short-term mission trips are not all that loving, even though they may have the best intentions. (And of course, other short-term mission trips can express exemplary love.)

Genuine love involves both aspects—a respect for the other person as someone we value plus reflecting on the best way to meet the specific needs the other person might have.

Affection (Heart)

That genuine love engages the heart is not at all controversial. It's where our culture is at. But this aspect of love still merits a few moments' reflection.

After all, there is no heartless, affection-free love.

We cannot love someone without also, in some sense, liking them.

This is why loving our neighbor, for example, can be so challenging. We don't always like our neighbors. So we sometimes think, "I'll at least show my love by being civil and sometimes even nice to them." But this is not love. Love always involves our affection.

Sometimes the affection part comes easily, and we don't have to wonder whether we can like the person. Other times, we really have to work at liking someone before we can love them. And if you love someone long enough and deeply enough, you're bound to experience both sides of that. And the people who love you will too.

This is why the mind and will are so much a part of love. Feelings come and go depending on situations and circumstances, both external and internal. Sometimes we have to force ourselves to think differently about another person if we are to love him or her. We can start by identifying or recalling two or three admirable traits.

Or if even that's too much, we might begin by replacing our dislike with pity. We might consider, for example, what circumstances or experiences have led the person to be "the way they are."

Isn't this how you sometimes overlook the flaws in people you already like?

Having genuine love for a person always means cultivating affection for him or her as a unique individual.

Sacrifice (Will)

It isn't truly love until we are willing to put it into action—to sacrifice something of ourselves for the other's good, whether time, energy, resources, or whatever. Love always expresses itself in sacrifice.

That's why one of the best ways to learn to love someone who is hard to love is to begin to make small sacrifices for that person.

You've heard it said that Christians are to love *everyone*. While there might be an element of truth in that, it can be misleading too.

The truth is, we simply can't love everyone the way Christ calls us to love people. There was only one man who could love that way. If you have somehow convinced yourself that you "love everyone," you have probably redefined the word *love* into something so vague, generic, or theoretical that it loses its meaning.

Despite popular opinion, Jesus didn't tell us to love everyone. He asked us to do something much more challenging: love our neighbor. Love those who live nearest to us. The people we encounter daily.

Love is always local. Support worthy overseas missions with your prayers and finances, but don't think that absolves you from learning to love the people next door. Start by learning to love your neighbor. Only when you master that can you begin to contemplate what it would mean to love someone in a different city or on the other side of the world.

How to Love God

Jesus said that preparing ourselves for eternal life in the kingdom means learning to love God with all our heart, soul, mind, and strength.

That's another way of saying we're to love with our thoughts (mind), emotions (heart), and actions (strength)—all three. The *soul* refers to the whole person.

Shape your thoughts, emotions, and actions toward loving God and you will learn to love him with your whole being.

There are two key things you can do to engage your mind, heart, and will in loving God.

Worship

To worship means to take some of the attention you typically lavish on yourself and lavish it on God instead.

There is a time for corporate worship, and we'll talk more about the crucial importance of worshipping with other people in chapter ten. But it is just as important that we worship God in the midst of our homes, workplaces, and neighborhoods.

I don't mean by this that you need to plan worship services at each of those locations. (Although there certainly wouldn't be any harm in it. In fact, having planned and participated in worship at all three places myself, I say, "Go for it.") What I'm talking about here is more personal. Learning to love God means making the effort to recognize and appreciate God's goodness, kindness, mercy, and other attributes right there in the busyness and stress of your day. And if you see God perform a mighty act, celebrate that too.

If God is as great as they say he is (and he is), then we can hardly confine our praise to a single hour per week. And if we've done the work of loving God throughout the week, then our weekend worship will be a summing up of the worship we've offered throughout the week and a gathering together in one place of all the praises of God's people.

In-the-moment worship is the only adequate way to express our full respect and admiration for God, and with a little effort, it can become second nature to us.

One way to do it is to choose a quality or characteristic of God that you admire. Write it down and keep it close to where you'll be working. Each time you see it, stop just a moment and contemplate the glory of God in that particular quality. And as you go through the day, pay attention for evidence of that quality. When you see it, speak or just think a simple sentence of praise for God.

The next day, choose another quality. And each day, add to your list of the things you love about God.

Some days, you won't be able to think of a new trait. That's perfectly OK. Go back to the list you've already made and start back at the beginning. Work your way through it again. This is only one of many ways to develop the habit of worshipping God with your mind.

Another way to worship God is to develop the habit of thankfulness. Take some time each day or even several times a day to pause and list three things for which you're grateful. Then, offer a quick, non-elaborate prayer of thanksgiving to God for his kindness in providing these things that bring joy or comfort (or whatever) to your life.

Submission or Obedience

Submitting to God means putting yourself at his service.

Sometimes people think of it as "letting God take control." But that's not precisely right. It's not about control for God; in fact, he wants you to be calling the shots. That's why he's written the Law on your heart: so you don't have to ask him what to do every step of the way. Doing the right thing comes naturally.

God's not on a power trip. After all, he shared his image and glory with you. And he's working to renew and restore his image in you. He doesn't want to micromanage your life; he merely wants you to learn to live well—for your own sake and for the sake of others.

At first, submission might be more an *expression* of our love for God than a way to *strengthen* our love for God. Jesus said, "If you love me, you will keep my commandments" (John 14:15). We submit to God out of gratitude for redeeming our lives.

But as we submit to his plan of redemption, he really does begin to put our lives back together.

Putting on faith, hope, and love—and putting off their opposites—are not bureaucratic regulations meant to make life miserable and unlivable. They are the key to living life the way that brings fulfillment, joy, and peace to you and those around you.

The more we obey and see the results of obedience, the more we see that God has our best interests at heart. And he knows what's best for us.

This, in turn, gives us one more thing to add to our list of things we love about God.

How to Love Your Neighbor

Loving others is complicated.

Some people seem easy to love. We find them enjoyable to be around; there is plenty about them to admire and respect.

But others, for whatever reason, are just more difficult.

Learning to live well involves learning to love your neighbor no matter how easy or difficult they are to love.

C. S. Lewis says that loving often begins with doing. The feeling comes later. Lewis writes, "Do not waste time bothering whether you 'love' your neighbor; act as if you did. As soon as we do this we find one of the great secrets. When you are behaving as if you loved someone, you will presently come to love him. . . . Whenever we do good to another self, just because it is a self, made (like us) by God, and desiring its own happiness as we desire ours, we shall have learned to love it a little more or, at least, to dislike it less."*

Behaving as if you love someone comes down to two key attitudes or actions.

Respect

Loving others begins with respect and admiration.

Too often we are self-centered in the way that we value or devalue other people. We judge them based on how they make us feel or what they can do for us. Sometimes we treat people well when we think they might be able to do something for us, and then we treat them differently when we find they are unwilling to deliver. This is not respect but manipulation.

Respect flows from a belief that the other person is intrinsically valuable simply because she was created by God, just as you were.

---

*C. S. Lewis, *Mere Christianity* (New York: MacMillan, 1952), 116.

If you want to learn to love someone, make a conscious effort to find something about the person that is admirable and worthy of respect. If you've racked your brain and still can't think of anything, you can at the very least treat him as a person who is created in the image of God, a candidate for divine redemption, and someone chosen for a unique role in God's redemption of the world—just as you are. Begin to see your neighbors from this biblical perspective and you'll have solid reasons to offer them your respect. After all, Jesus knows everything you do about them, and he laid down his life to secure their redemption.

Treating someone respectfully begins with acknowledging her existence. You cannot respect someone whom you ignore or with whom you refuse to spend time. Respect always involves giving the person the time she needs and often giving her the time she desires, even when you don't feel like it. Respect also means speaking and acting toward the other person with kindness and gentleness, avoiding sarcasm and other kinds of cutting remarks. In other words, treating someone with respect means using care in the way you interact with that person rather than treating him whatever way suits your emotions at the moment.

This is different from being formal in your relationships, but it certainly could feel stiff and awkward at first.

Like nearly every other aspect of spiritual growth, loving your neighbor involves turning your attention away from yourself and your desires and turning it toward what the other person needs. Growing in love always means growing in respect for the other.

Submission or Service

Submission is at the heart of any relationship of love. But there is much confusion about what it means to submit, and who should submit to whom, and how one should submit.

So let's begin with the fact that the apostle Paul says all Christians should submit to one another (Eph. 5:21). In other words, submission involves mutuality; it goes both ways.

Christian submission is not about letting the other person dominate or control your interactions or relationships. It's not about burying your personality, needs, or desires so that another person gets his or her way.

Instead, submission is about taking into account what others need and what is best for them and everyone and then acting toward that end.

When we truly love others, we humble ourselves, "count others more significant than [ourselves]" (Phil. 2:3), and put their needs first. We do not genuinely love someone unless we are moved to act on his or her behalf, setting aside our own convenience and desires in order to make a positive difference in that person's life.

It should be clear that I'm not advocating for relationships where one person dominates and the other person submits. Quite the contrary; such relationships are demeaning and dangerous. I'm advocating for relationships in the church and the home where both believers submit to one another, as Scripture commands.

Genuine love involves serving and submitting. As with submission to God, submission to another Christian may at first be an expression of love rather than a way to grow your love. But as C. S. Lewis said, the way to grow love is often to act is if you already do love. As you choose to serve and submit for the purpose of loving the other person in Christ, you will quite naturally grow in your love for that person.

Five Keys for Redemptive Relationships

We are broken people trying to live and work with other broken people. Our relationships will likely always reflect some degree of brokenness. You will sometimes hurt me and I will sometimes hurt you. It's part of the curse of living in a fallen, broken world. Yet part of the beauty of relationships is that they always contain the hope of redemption. God can put people back together again, and he can restore relationships. I believe he wants to work through you and me to make it happen.

There are no scientific formulas when it comes to relationships. They hold much more mystery than a mathematical equation. But there are some key attitudes and behaviors that will set the tone for healing, whether in your own relationships or as you care for others.

Presence. Few things are more powerful in a relationship than our presence. By our words and actions, we can communicate that "I am with you and will continue to be with you."

Gentleness. When we treat others with gentleness, it signals acceptance, not of the sin or brokenness but of the person. Such gentleness is a gift that helps open the door to redemption of the relationship.

Attention. A person who has been wounded needs others to understand the depth of his pain. That's why genuine, nonjudgmental listening is a pathway to healing in a relationship.

Forgiveness. I don't know if there is a more powerful force in the world than forgiveness. No one deserves to be forgiven; it is always a gift. If we want to have lasting relationships, we need to cultivate a readiness to forgive.

Hope. The hope needed to restore broken relationships is found in a God who prefers to redeem and restore rather then condemn and destroy. We can have hope for sustainable, loving relationships, because God is working through Jesus Christ to fix what's broken. Those who choose to follow his pathway to holiness will find not only that their sins are forgiven but also that their relationships are being restored.

We seek faith and hope because they are the foundation of our love for God and others. And as we grow in love for God and others, our presence, gentleness, attention, forgiveness, and hope—all expressions of our love for God and others—work together to bring healing to our relationships.

Now we're really starting to reflect his glory by living well!

Personal Reflection

1. What things make it challenging for you to love God?
2. What are some reasons to love God that you sometimes overlook or forget?
3. What makes it challenging for you to love a particular neighbor?
4. What are some admirable characteristics of that neighbor that you don't often focus on?
5. What relationship do you have in your life right now that needs to experience healing?
6. Which of the five keys for redemptive relationships might you need to focus on in that relationship?

Next Steps

1. Choose one quality or attribute of God to recognize, appreciate, or celebrate this week. Find a way that works for you to frequently remember and praise God for this quality.
2. Make an effort to notice at least one way in which God is active

in your life this week. Be sure to praise him in the moment as well as bring the praise with you to weekend worship.

3. Identify one neighbor or coworker for whom you need to grow in love. Find a small way to serve that person this week.

4. Choose one relationship in your life that needs to experience healing. Using the five keys from this chapter, take one small step toward redeeming that relationship this week.

Part Three

IN A POCKET OF
THE KINGDOM

*Jesus came among us to show and teach the life for which we
were made. . . . By relying on his word and presence we are
enabled to reintegrate the little realm that makes up our life
into the infinite rule of God.*
—Dallas Willard

Chapter 9
SCRIPTURE

Interpretation of Scripture is always a communal act.
—David Fitch

I confess. I don't read my Bible every day.

Don't get me wrong. I've done plenty of Bible reading in my lifetime.

But as a general rule, I don't read it every day. It just doesn't seem to work best that way for me.

It's worth noting at this point that the Bible doesn't tell us to read it every day. It's more like "common wisdom" that reading the Bible daily is the ideal. The activity advocated in passages like Deuteronomy 6:6–9, Joshua 1:8, and Psalm 1:2 is actually quite different from what we think of as "daily Bible reading," especially since most people at the time did not have a personal copy of the Scriptures. Any "reading" of Scripture most people did in those days was mostly listening to Scripture in community. Instead, these passages instruct people to do something even more helpful and important: to meditate daily on how to fulfill the Law, or in other words, how to demonstrate faith, hope, and love for God and others in daily life.

Some might say a lack of daily Bible reading is a sign of immaturity. But it may say more about reading style.

Most Bible reading plans, in my opinion, are designed for people who don't like to read, or at least, they don't like to read the Bible. The plans parcel out Bible reading in small bites that often don't follow any discernible story or flow of thought. It takes one to three years or more to read the whole Bible. Imagine trying to read any other book that way.

Instead of rationing it out, I try to read the Bible like I love it.

When I begin to read a series like The Lord of the Rings or The Hunger Games, I devour the books from cover to cover. I read several chapters at a time. I speed through each book to get the flow of the story from beginning to conflict to climax to resolution. When I'm done, I might go back and review a certain part because it meant something to me or because I want to see if I understand it any better now that I know the whole story.

And then I put the book away for a while. It sits there in the back of my mind as I process what I've read.

If it's a really good book, I know I'll be coming back to it. Again and again. Because I want to relive the story.

My kids think I know a lot about The Lord of the Rings, and I do. But it's not because I read The Lord of the Rings every day. And it's not because I've spent hours analyzing key passages. It's because it draws me in, and I keep returning to relive the story.

That's how I tend to read the Bible. I return to it over and over again so that the flow of the story is written on my heart. Then I come back to reread certain parts because they meant something to me or because I want to understand them better. And then I might not even touch my Bible for a few days. But even on those days when I don't touch it, it's still percolating inside me, shaping and guiding me, because it has become a part of me. I'm daily meditating on how to live out the story of God's word in my life.

I can imagine some questions.

Kevin, are you saying people shouldn't read their Bibles every day?

No, I'm saying that everyone should find a way of reading the Bible that fits their personality and reading style. Everyone doesn't have to fit into the same template. If you're reading the Bible every day and grasping the big picture, and if your reading sessions don't feel mostly like drudgery or discipline, then by all means, keep doing what you're doing. But if daily reading is a struggle, then you might try another approach.

Kevin, aren't you afraid you're giving people permission to not read the Bible?

No, not at all. I'm trying to give people permission to read it in the way that will have the greatest impact on their lives rather than merely checking off a daily reading because that's what they're "supposed" to do.

Kevin, don't you think you'd be better off if you read your Bible every day?

I don't know. Maybe. Probably. It would mean that I'm drawn to the Bible even more than I already am. But realistically I know that the way I read the Bible best is in large chunks, many chapters at a time. That's not something I have the luxury of doing on a daily basis. So I'm content knowing that I've found a pattern that sustains me, even though it's not the typical daily Bible reading plan.

Personal Bible reading is an important part of the way that God re-creates our souls and helps us learn to live well. But what I want us to consider in this chapter is that Bible reading is not a solitary activity. As important as it is to find a way to read the Bible on your own, it's just as important to read the Bible with others—within a functioning pocket of the kingdom.

Reading the Bible in community stretches and challenges us in ways that personal Bible reading rarely does. It binds us to the community and shapes our souls toward holiness.

Four Ways the Bible Speaks into Our Lives

One reason people sometimes have trouble connecting with Scripture is that they don't understand what kind of book it is, how it works, and what it's designed to do for you.

The Bible is not a book of answers to the questions you have about life. Sorry. It might be nice if there were such a book. But the Bible isn't it. Sure, the Bible contains answers, but they're not usually the answers to the precise questions you're asking. The Bible answers its own questions, not the questions we might bring to it.

And the Bible is not a rulebook that tells you what to do and how to respond in every situation. There are certainly bits of specific instruction about what to do and what not to do, but the Bible is not interested in micromanaging your life. Instead, it wants to shape your soul so that you are more guided by the virtues written on your heart than a paper list of legal regulations.

Nor is the Bible a guide for how to get to heaven. The Bible offers hope for life after death, but it seems much more interested in what you do with your life.

There are many true things that can be said about the Bible, so please don't take the following as an exhaustive list. I leave that to the commentaries and systematic theologies. But I want to share four truths about Scripture and how it speaks in our lives so that we can live well in pockets of the kingdom.

Community Text

Sometimes it seems like the Bible was written especially for *you*. It speaks directly to your soul. But it's surprisingly important to keep in mind that the Bible was written for a specific community within a specific set of ancient cultures.

It was written with certain assumptions or presuppositions in mind:

1. Monotheism: there is one God who is Lord over all creation.
2. Election: God has chosen a particular group of people to be his glory-bearers in the world.
3. Eschatology: God has a plan to fix everything that is broken in the world.

N. T. Wright has demonstrated that these were the basic theological beliefs of a particular ancient community: historic Judaism.* And the beliefs and culture of this ancient community form the background of every text in the Old and New Testaments.

The Bible is not primarily an apologetic text written for the purpose of convincing people to believe. It is a community text written for those who already do, with the intent that it should shape the lives, culture, and mission of a group of people who seek the one, true God. The Bible will certainly shape your personal life; however, its primary goal is to shape the life of pockets of the kingdom where Christ-followers are learning to reflect his glory by living well.

Revelatory Text

Christians have always understood the Scriptures to be more than a mere historical record. The Bible reveals God's thoughts, God's purposes, God's plan.

---

*See section 2 of N. T. Wright, *Paul: In Fresh Perspective* (Minneapolis, MN: Fortress, 2005).

In some way that we do not fully comprehend, God inspired the writers of Scripture so that we have in the Bible the written revelation of God. It contains precisely the words the community of God's people needed in order to understand God's narrative of redemption and their place within it.

God still speaks through these same Scriptures to each new generation of believers to shape us into the people he has called us to be and to guide us on the task of seeking God's redemption in all of our relationships.

This is some of what theologians mean when they say that the Bible is God's special revelation to humanity. God has revealed himself and his plan to those who seek him through the pages of Scripture. What we find in the Bible is sufficient and reliable to lead us on the pathway to redemption and eternal life in God's kingdom.

Much more could be said about the Bible as God's revelation, but I leave that to the commentaries and systematic theologies. The key thing is to know that God reveals his plan to us through Scripture.

Unfinished Narrative

The Bible comes to us not as a book of doctrine or systematic theology, nor as a set of practical principles, but as a story. It is the true narrative that traces God's plan of redemption from beginning to end.

It is possible to summarize the story and quickly communicate the main themes. In fact, I did some of that in chapter 6. Doctrine and systematic theology are human attempts to summarize the story of Scripture and communicate it in objective, propositional truths. This is a worthy pursuit. But we must never forget that the Bible did not come to us as a doctrine textbook or a series of bullet points about objective truth. It came to us as a story, and it was always intended that we encounter it as a story. Even the parts that are not pure story, such as the psalms, take place within the context of a story and are best understood when we keep that in mind.

But as a story, the Bible is incomplete. It starts at the beginning with creation and the fall of humankind into brokenness. It traces God's plan of redemption through Israel, Jesus, and the early church. But then it jumps ahead to describe the end of the story and what final redemption will look like.

In other words, it leaves a great big old gap in the story.

And your life and mine fall within the gap.

The church is called to bridge the gap—to live out the gospel that Jesus is Lord and Redeemer and to reflect his glory until he returns.

Redemptive Text

Scripture narrates the story of our redemption, but it is also part of the means by which God accomplishes our redemption. As we read Scripture in community with other believers, God works through it to shape our lives and to accomplish the redemption and restoration that Jesus has already paid for on the cross.

Not to belabor the point, but the Bible is not only the message about how we can be saved and become like Christ; it is also part of what brings about our transformation.

This is why Scripture is not an optional part of spiritual growth. It is one of the normal and necessary means of a person's growth in authentic holiness.

There is power in God's word.

The Bible, along with the finished work of Christ and the operation of the Holy Spirit, changes lives. Those who want to follow Jesus and learn to live well can only do so by becoming people of the Word.

Three Ways Scripture Shapes God's People

The Bible was not written as a mystical, sacred text to impart random, hidden, secret knowledge. Does God ever reveal himself to a person through the Bible this way? Maybe. He certainly could. But he won't reveal anything in this manner that couldn't have been learned by reading Scripture for what it is: a redemptive, revelatory, unfinished narrative written for the formation and guidance of the community of God's covenant.

Scripture shapes our lives in three primary ways.

Revealing Our Heritage

First, like any newborn child, we are born into a particular spiritual family, one that has a rich history and heritage. Or more accurately, we are *adopted* into this spiritual family. And having been claimed, we are naturally curious about our roots. We want to know what kind of family it is that has adopted us. Why do they do this or that? Why is this thing expected of me?

And so we begin to take an interest in our heritage. The Bible is the sourcebook for the rich history of the spiritual family into which we've been adopted. We can't truly understand the family of Christ, with all of its history and expectations, without spending time in Scripture.

Defining Our Culture

Scripture also defines the culture of the Christian community, identifying values that shape the way Christians live and relate to others within pockets of the kingdom.

The Virtues

The Christian virtues—faith, hope, and love—become the key values of any truly Christian culture. Not only do they guide the choices we make as individuals, but they also guard, protect, and nurture our relationships, both within the church and with those who are not a part of the Christian community. Practicing Christian faith, hope, and love in community helps us to avoid, or at least work around, the pain and brokenness that mars so many relationships. Scripture plays a key role in shaping and defining this culture of healthy relationships.

The Fruit

Other values, including the fruit of the Spirit, build on the foundation of the three virtues. The apostle Paul identifies nine varieties of fruit that are found in the life of a believer who is being shaped by the Holy Spirit toward authentic holiness: "love, joy, peace, patience, kindness, goodness, faithfulness, gentleness, self-control" (Gal. 5:22–23). He contrasts these with the "works of the flesh" that characterize someone that is not walking in the Spirit. These include "sexual immorality, impurity, sensuality, idolatry, sorcery, enmity, strife, jealousy, fits of anger, rivalries, dissensions, divisions, envy, drunkenness, orgies, and things like these" (Gal. 5:19–21).

The culture of the Christian community is to continually put off the one (works of the flesh) while putting on the other (fruit of the Spirit), as if you were changing out of one set of clothing for another.

In his letter to the Romans, Paul said that Christians are to "put on the Lord Jesus Christ, and make no provision for the flesh, to gratify its desires" (Rom. 13:14). This is not something that happens automatically or effortlessly in the life of the Christian. We must cooperate with the Spirit. And one of the tools we're given to help with the transformation is the Word of God.

As with the virtues, adding the fruit of the Spirit to our lives will have a dramatic impact on the way that we relate to both Christians and those who don't know Christ.

The Examples

Another way that Scripture defines the culture of Christianity is by providing plenty of examples, both positive and negative, of what it means to live a life of authentic holiness. Since Scripture is not a book of doctrine but a story, it helps us see what it looks like to live a life that is characterized by faith, hope, love, and the fruit of the Spirit through the lives of people like Abraham, Deborah, Esther, and Paul. We can also see the devastating results of rejecting the pathway of holiness in the lives of people like Saul and Solomon, and so many of the kings described in the books of Kings and Chronicles.

The true stories of real characters within the true story of Scripture will shape our lives if we allow them to, and they will give us wisdom as we pursue the pathway of holiness.

Guiding Our Pathway

A third way Scripture shapes us is by calling us into mission. You are to become a certain kind of person and be part of a certain kind of community, because God has a certain kind of role for you to play in his kingdom.

The Bible, along with the Holy Spirit, shapes your character and creates within you the life of Christ so that you can then participate in the mission to which he has called you. And most often, this happens as you read the Bible together with others in community, a pocket of God's kingdom.

We will say much more in chapter 12 about the nature of that mission; for now, it's enough to note that Scripture has something to say not only about who we are becoming but also about what kinds of things are to occupy our time.

How to Read Scripture

Throughout church history, followers of Jesus have acknowledged that a regular diet of Scripture is an essential part of shaping the believer's life for following Christ. For the Christian who wants to grow toward authentic holiness, practicing the life of Jesus until it becomes second nature, there is no substitute for gaining mastery in the text that tells the story.

Read the Way You Read

As I mentioned earlier, I only recently figured out that my Bible reading (and my walk with Christ) would benefit greatly by my approaching Bible reading like I do any other story. I'm not saying that this is the only way to read the Bible. What I am saying is that you need to find a Bible study plan that fits your best way of reading and learning and one that helps you see the entire flow of Scripture from beginning to end.

My current favorite plan takes me through the entire Bible in ninety days. That doesn't mean I read the Bible four times in a year, but I do end up reading through the Bible more quickly and more often than I would at just a few verses or a couple of chapters a day. Ironically, I find this less challenging than reading random chapters from Genesis, Psalms, Isaiah, Matthew, and Romans in the same day. This Bible reading plan fits my style of reading. Find the one that fits yours and then dive in.

Read for the Story

The Christian Scriptures are in a different category from other mystical, sacred texts. We should not approach them seeking some magical encounter where secret truth is revealed to us. While God can certainly reveal himself in any way he chooses, the Bible was designed to be read and understood for what it is: a story, not a magical portal to secret knowledge.

However you choose to read Scripture, it is essential that you connect with the story that ties everything together from Genesis to Revelation. Focus on grasping the overarching narrative, and then try to understand how each passage you encounter fits into the larger story. This larger story was summarized for you in the first part of this book, and that summary will help you find your way into Scripture; however, it is not intended to be a substitute for reading the complete story. Read the story to understand its characters and follow the twists and turns of the plot. It is only as you engage with the story of Scripture for yourself that the Bible will begin to shape your life and mission.

So read the Bible for understanding, not for sudden, unexplained insight. Insights will come, but mostly as you do the work of reading and understanding. And that means grasping the overall story, not just the few verses in front of you at the moment.

Read to Gain Wisdom

As you read the Bible in this way, your goal is first understanding and then wisdom. Pray for and seek wisdom as you read the Scriptures.

Wisdom is deeper than mere understanding. Wisdom is the ability to make decisions that take you further down the pathway of authentic holiness rather than taking a detour or returning to a dead-end pathway. Wisdom is the ability to make decisions that strengthen healthy relationships rather than breaking them. Wisdom is the ability to make decisions that advance the mission of Christ and the kingdom rather than obstructing or tearing down his redemptive work.

We only gain wisdom as the narrative, characters, and themes of

Scripture seep into every pore of our being and shape us into the image of Christ.

Read in Community

Much of your Bible reading and understanding will come as a result of your personal, private reading, but it is just as important that you read Scripture in community with other believers. By reading and studying Scripture with other Christians, you gain from the collective wisdom of the body of Christ. You are sharpened, challenged, and corrected—sometimes by those with many more years spent walking the pathway of holiness and other times by those who are new to the faith and thus bring a different perspective.

Community reading of Scripture is essential. Left to ourselves, we can easily misunderstand and misinterpret this grand story that was written at another time and in different languages. Reading in community helps us avoid blind spots in our understanding of Scripture and the Christian life.

We can also read in community with saints who have gone before us. Christians of previous decades and centuries have left us a rich treasure in their understanding and interpretation of Scripture. We do well to pay attention to this valuable treasure. The writings of our predecessors will challenge, correct, and guide our reading of Scripture. We may sometimes disagree on certain points even with those whom we greatly respect. But the least we can do is listen and understand, letting their wisdom shape and guide our interpretation.

Again, the primary goal of our reading as Christians is the pursuit of wisdom, the ability to make decisions consistently that will keep us on the pathway toward authentic holiness in life and mission. The result of this pursuit, though we cannot accomplish it ourselves, will be the ultimate redemption of our souls.

Personal Reflection

1. When have you experienced God speaking to you through Scripture?
2. In what ways has Scripture shaped your life?
3. How do you see yourself and your church community fitting into the unfinished narrative of Scripture?
4. Is your current approach to reading Scripture helping you connect with the overall story? What might you need to change?
5. How has reading Scripture in community been a part of your life? How might it play a more important role?
6. How might you go about connecting more with the heritage and culture of God's people through Scripture?

Next Steps

1. Spend some time evaluating how well your current approach to Scripture is helping you to connect with the heritage, culture, and unfinished narrative of God's people. Consider whether another plan might be a better fit for you at this point.
2. If you are not currently reading Scripture with other Christians, make plans to find or create a group for this purpose.
3. When you read Scripture—either alone or with a group— develop a habit of asking, "How does this passage fit into the larger story of God's redemption?" Wrestle with the question until you think you know the answer.
4. When you gain insight or a bit of wisdom from Scripture, don't keep it to yourself. Share it with another person or group so they can benefit from it too. Perhaps they'll be able to shed even more light on the subject.

Chapter 10

WORSHIP

Worship . . . imprints on our whole being
the reality that we study.
—Dallas Willard

I looked, and behold, a door standing open in heaven!" (Rev. 4:1). Imagine what that must have looked like.

John was imprisoned on an island in the Mediterranean. He had been such a faithful witness for Jesus that he became a thorn in Caesar's side, so he was sent into exile.

One Sunday morning, John had a vision of the risen Lord Jesus. At Jesus' instruction, John wrote down some of the content of that vision in a book which we know today as the Revelation or the Apocalypse (Rev. 1:9–11). After first writing down several messages from Jesus to seven ancient churches, John began to describe what he saw that day.

It was like someone had left the door of heaven open so John could look within.

Then Jesus invited John to step inside so he could be shown "what must take place after this" (Rev. 4:1). John suddenly found himself in the throne room of heaven.

There, John got a glimpse of the worship taking place in God's presence. There were twenty-four elders, seven spirits, and four living creatures all offering praise, saying, "Holy, holy, holy, is the Lord God Almighty, who was and is and is to come!" (4:8) and "Worthy are you, our Lord and God, to receive glory and honor and power, for you created all things, and by your will they existed and were created" (v. 11)

This is the essence of worship: entering into God's presence and expressing God's worth, both because of who he is and because of what he has done.

Many things about worship are controversial, but there is nothing controversial about this: humanity was made to worship God and give him glory. We are called to do this by reflecting his glory throughout all creation.

We talked in the first section about the veil that separates heaven and earth and how, at certain times, the veil opens so that heaven touches earth, a holy intersection.

Genuine worship can be one of those times and places.

When we worship God, we join with the elders, the spirits, and the creatures in heaven, who are continually offering their praise to God.

I said earlier that Christians can and should offer worship to God at any time and wherever they happen to be. But private worship is not enough. The story of God's redemption, from the beginning, has been about the redemption of a *community*.

One of God's greatest accomplishments is the formation of the community of redemption, made of people from every time, place, culture, and ethnicity. We cannot reflect the glory of this accomplishment by ourselves. We must come together with God's people in corporate worship if we are to fully reflect God's glory as we were called to do.

Four Postures of True Worship

Christians need not go to a particular place or even look toward a certain hill to offer worship that is acceptable to God. Instead, the Spirit is to be found wherever two or three believers in Christ are gathered together. True worship arises from the hearts and lives of people who have submitted themselves to Christ. It involves four postures of the worshipper toward God.

Respond

When Christians come to God in worship, we never do so as the initiator. It was not our idea to worship God, and we do not spontaneously decide to do so out of the goodness of our hearts. Our worship is always a response. It's a response to God's invitation and command to worship him. It's a response to his mighty works, his position in the world, his great love for us, his mercy, his grace, and his work of redemption in our lives.

We don't worship God because of who we are but because of who he is. In fact, we are not even able to respond in worship apart from God's grace in our lives. Or to put it another way, our worship is to be a reflection of his glory. We are not the source of worship; he is. Our worship is merely a reflection back to God of the many ways in which his glory fills the earth.

This is one reason why we cannot worship God in whatever way we choose, thinking only of what suits our personal preference or style. We worship at God's invitation, so we must worship him in the way that he desires.

This is also why we should not be too quick to dismiss styles of worship that seem foreign to our preferences or culture. God's glory fills the whole earth, including every culture and people group. God's glory is reflected in more ways than you can imagine. Be jealous for

God to receive his glory more than you are to preserve your preferred style of worship.

After all, worship is a response. It is about God and not us.

Repent

When Christians come to God in worship, we must always do so with an attitude of repentance. Having said that, let me quickly add that I do not mean what many people think of when they hear the word *repentance*.

There is a strong, long-standing tradition within the church that revolves around deep introspection and confession of sin. Supposedly, a Christian should spend significant time and energy reflecting not only on her actions but also her innermost thoughts and motives to see if anything at all is out of sync with the way of Christ. The idea is that a person must search out and confess every little sinful inclination that may be hindering her walk with Christ.

Many Christians live in fear of harboring some unknown sinful thought or motivation; they bring a tremendous amount of unnecessary guilt upon themselves as people who are part of God's covenant of grace. A healthy amount of self-reflection and confession has its place, but many modern Christians go overboard to the point of living in fear and guilt. They could never comprehend claiming to be blameless like Job, or without conscious sin like David, or perfect in keeping the law like Paul.

In other words, they have become consumed by a modern obsession with the inward life rather than adopting the more biblical perspective of judging their lives by their actions. Not that thoughts, motivations, and feelings are unimportant; they shape our actions. But ultimately, the question is: What do your thoughts and feelings lead you to do?

The kind of introspection and confession I've just described is not what I mean by repentance. So what could the word mean?

Repentance always means to turn *away* from something *toward* something, and generally, the Greek word *metanoia* relates to the thing in which you put your trust or hope.

When we come to worship, we should turn away from all the things we are tempted to hope and trust in, and we should turn to the only One who is truly worthy of our trust and hope: the God who has revealed himself to us as Father, Son, and Holy Spirit. As we worship, we consciously turn our mind, soul, and strength away from whatever offers false hope and toward the one true and living hope.

Celebrate

When Christians come to God in worship, we are moved to celebrate his mighty acts. In other words, worship is about praising God for who he is as he reveals himself to us through what he does.

God's mighty works fall broadly into three major categories: creation, providence, and redemption. We can never exhaust the honor and thanksgiving that is due to God in any of these areas.

We can celebrate the creative impulse of God that led to the creation of every magnificent vista, each beautiful relationship, and the never-ending capacity for exploration and discovery within the world God created. We can be forever grateful that God provides everything we need at so many different levels. And we can celebrate with all of God's people the amazing truth that God did not cast our broken, scarred lives away but chose instead to redeem and restore us.

As we reflect on God's marvelous works, we also grasp more and more of his character.

Our praise for God's character can fall broadly into three major categories: God's love, his righteousness, and his wisdom.

It is God's love for his creation that moved him to set in motion a plan to redeem us. It is God's wisdom that conceived the plan that would undo all the brokenness that resulted from humanity's sin. And it's God righteousness that gives us the hope and confidence that he will be faithful to his covenant to the end.

Christian worship is about the celebration of these mighty acts of God along with the excellences of his character.

Submit

Finally, our worship is not genuine Christian worship unless we come with a submissive attitude. Christian worship takes place in the presence of a sovereign God. We gather to worship our King, Jesus Christ, and the only proper way to worship the King is with an attitude of humble submission.

I have always loved the passage from J. R. R. Tolkien's *The Return of the King* when the hobbit Pippin kneels before the steward of Gondor, Lord Denethor, and pledges his unending service to the realm of Gondor. Even though Pippin pledges himself to an unworthy lord, it is an unforgettable picture of true humility and submission to one who is greater.

We come to the service of our Lord as less than a hobbit, offering our services to a mighty King who has need of nothing. Yet he desires our service, and the only proper response is our submission.

This is one of the reasons I have long maintained that there is no place for the modern aura of "cool" in Christian worship. The first time I shared this thought many years ago on a Christian Internet discussion board, I was quickly ridiculed for being "jealous" of worship leaders who were cooler than I. Maybe I was, but the fact is, no one is "cool" in the presence of a Sovereign Lord. God does not honor our attitudes of superiority. The only proper attitude for worship—from

leaders or worshippers—is the humble submission you would demonstrate if you were invited to step through the open doorway into the
throne room of heaven.

Two Ways That Worship Shapes Us

It is common for people in the church today, especially the evangelical church, to evaluate a church and even each worship service according to whether they "got anything out of it." By this, they usually mean
either (1) some inspirational thought to help them on their way, or
(2) some nugget of application that will help them in a certain area of
life, or (3) to put it simply and crassly, some entertainment value.

While there is absolutely nothing wrong with receiving one or
more of the above from worship, there are at least two problems with
expecting it. The first is that worship is not primarily about us but
about God. It is about the worshipper only insomuch as we humbly
submit ourselves before God to repent and celebrate his redemption
in our lives.

A second reason why we should not expect to "get something out
of" worship every week is, quite simply, that it is not how worship
works.

Unquestionably, worship shapes our lives significantly, but not primarily by giving us some thought or experience we can latch onto for
the coming week. Worship works on the soul of a believer in a more
indirect fashion.

There is something you must do: participate in worship with all
your heart, soul, mind, and strength. There is also something that
God does. You must do your part and then trust that he will do his.
It does not happen in a moment, and you may not realize it is happening. But one day, you will be able to look back and see how God
has shaped you through worship.

More Like God

As we participate in genuine worship, over time God shapes us so that we become more like him.

You have probably heard it said that you become like what you worship. There is a lot of truth to that. The person who idolizes a certain musician tends to sing or play like that musician. The person who looks up to a particular baseball player assumes a similar batting stance. The person who enjoys a famous comedian tries to adopt that comedian's sense of wit and timing. You get the idea. When we celebrate, worship, or adore someone, we tend to become more like that person, at least in the areas that we most admire and often without even thinking about it.

It is the same when we worship God. As we give ourselves to God in genuine worship—responding, repenting, celebrating, and submitting—we find that we are gradually becoming more like him. His values are becoming our values. His character is becoming our character. His interests are becoming our interests.

This movement toward God does not occur because we are "trying" to become more like God, but because in worship we are applying ourselves to a discipline that the Holy Spirit uses to shape us.

That is not to say that simply going to church each Sunday will make you a better follower of Christ (though the kind of church you attend and what goes on during its worship service matters greatly). However, as you genuinely respond, repent, celebrate, and submit in worship, the Holy Spirit will progressively shape your soul in ways that are beyond your understanding.

More Human

God also uses worship to make us more fully human. Since we were created in his image and for the purpose of reflecting his glory, becoming more like God means at the same time becoming more genuinely human. As we engage in worshipping God, the Holy Spirit shapes us so that we draw ever closer to fulfilling the purpose for which God created us.

People have often thought that being human is roughly the opposite of being God. Humans are finite; God is infinite. We are sinful; God is holy. We mess up; God is perfect. We break things; God puts them back together.

To an extent, these statements are true. But, except for the matter of infinity, they are true only of *fallen* humanity. When God created humankind, he had something much different in mind: a creature that perfectly reflected his character and glory.

We are used to equating being human with messing up. But in reality, being fully human means being redeemed and restored so that we begin to fulfill God's original purpose for us. Genuine worship is one of the means by which God, in some mysterious way beyond our understanding, accomplishes his work of restoration.

We are never *less* human than when we put ourselves on a pedestal and expect God to either do our bidding or else go away. We are never *more* human than when we respond, repent, celebrate, and submit to him in worship.

Four Ways to Participate in Worship

As I hinted in the previous section, not all Christian worship is created equal, and since worship itself shapes us, the content of our worship matters. In this section, I want to describe some of the elements of worship and how they can and should cultivate life-change in us.

Before doing so, however, I want to offer a word of caution. It is not my desire that you become dissatisfied or discouraged with the style or content of worship at the church you're attending and decide to begin looking for a church that "does worship better." I firmly believe that as long as the worship service exalts the God of the Bible, the most significant factor in how worship transforms you is what you bring to the table: your mind, heart, and will.

So, don't worry so much about whether your church "measures up" to the ideal I describe below. Mine doesn't, even though I was involved in planning our church's worship from the beginning. Every church is an expression of its members' strengths and weaknesses, and you will not find a church that worships perfectly.

So, don't use my suggestions to pressure your pastor into making changes in the worship service. Instead, use them as a guide for how you personally might think about your participation in worship, whatever style your congregation employs.

Of course, I hope your church will learn to cultivate worship that most effectively transforms people into disciples who are guided by their growing faith, hope, and love (just as I hope the same for my own church). If you are involved in leading worship, perhaps what follows can help you make adjustments so that worship can encourage life change. In any case, my purpose for sharing these thoughts is to help you prepare for meaningful, life-transforming worship no matter what your church's style.

Liturgy

I use the word *liturgy* intentionally, even though I know that to some it will sound foreign, and to others, it will suggest something formal and stiff.

But the latter is a misconception. A church's liturgy is simply its pattern or order of worship. It may be formal or informal, but every church has one. It's not a question of whether your church follows a liturgy but what *kind* of liturgy it follows.

Some churches follow a detailed liturgy that prescribes when to sit and stand, what the minister should say and how the people should respond, which Scriptures should be read and which passage the minister should use to preach. Other liturgies are much more barebones and relaxed: worship set, Scripture reading, prayer, another worship set, special music, sermon, and offering.

While many churches may vary their typical worship pattern in minor ways from week to week, most follow some kind of template. That pattern, whatever it looks like, is your church's liturgy.

The liturgy helps the congregation understand what is going on in worship and how to respond. As a worshipper, your job is to understand each component of worship so you can enter into it with your whole mind, heart, and will.

Even if your congregation has a relaxed liturgy or order of worship, you can still make an effort to understand the intent of the worship flow and even privately add elements to your personal experience of public worship. For example, perhaps your congregation has lots of music but no time set aside for repentance. You can privately enter into a time of repentance during the singing or prayer.

In addition to the order of worship, most churches use at least some elements of the traditional church calendar to guide their worship, if only to observe Christmas and Easter. The traditional church calendar has guided countless Christians over the centuries through an annual pilgrimage from Christ's birth through his passion and resurrection to his ascension to heaven. Paying attention to the church calendar, even if it's not a major emphasis of your church's worship, is an excellent way to add depth to your personal worship and enhance your spiritual growth.

Storytelling

Christian worship has always included a certain amount of story-telling. The only way we can adequately celebrate God's mighty acts, for example, is to tell the story of what God has done. We tell one another about his works of creation, providence, and redemption.

In many churches, the congregation engages in storytelling primarily through song. We allow the hymn writers of the past or contemporary songwriters to gather up the praises of his people into a song that we can sing together, declaring the story of redemption that God is writing in the world.

In many congregations, members are also encouraged to share their stories or testimonies about how God is working in their lives. These stories encourage us, but they also teach us to see God working in our own lives in similar ways.

The preaching of God's Word is another aspect of storytelling. While not every minister approaches the sermon as a story, part of this book's emphasis is that the whole of Scripture forms a story. Even if the minister in your church doesn't always show how the day's Scripture passage fits into the Bible's overall narrative, you know enough now to bring that aspect of storytelling to the table in your private experience of public worship. You can fill in the gaps yourself or make a note to study this or that aspect of the message later to see how it fits into God's overarching narrative.

Scripture reading also brings storytelling into the worship service. Bible reading serves as more than a text for the message. The reading of Scripture in public worship—not just in short segments but lengthier passages as well—is a significant aspect of the storytelling that ought to take place in corporate worship.

Stories are perhaps the primary way we understand our place in the universe. That's why it is critical that we emphasize the telling of

God's story in our worship, so his story continues to give meaning to our lives.

Prayer

Corporate worship also presents the opportunity for God's people to join their hearts in prayer. While personal, private prayer is certainly an important aspect of growing in your walk with Christ, it is no substitute for praying together with God's people in community. Many churches today deemphasize public prayer, whether because it seems to break the flow of worship or because privacy concerns may arise from mentioning personal needs in a public setting. Nevertheless, the Bible teaches us to pray corporately. As we enter into corporate prayer with all of our heart, soul, mind, and strength, it shapes us in ways that are beyond our capacity to understand.

Sacraments

Again, I realize I am using a word that might be controversial, but I intentionally embrace the word *sacraments* because it communicates that something is going on in these special observances of the church that brings heaven and earth together.

Churches differ as to what and how many sacraments there are, but churches in every tradition agree that Jesus affirmed the practice of two special observances: baptism and communion. Baptism relates to the beginning of a believer's walk with Christ while communion relates more to the ongoing need for Christ in our lives. Communion is sometimes also known as the Lord's Supper or the Lord's Table or the Eucharist. Whatever you call it, communion is another of those practices that, in some way beyond our capacity to describe, invites the Holy Spirit to re-create us in authentic holiness.

Some churches practice communion infrequently, as little as once per year. At our church, we practice it every week.

Jesus said that as often as we observe communion, we proclaim his death and resurrection. This meal the Lord gave us to eat together is so filled with significance that in order to cover it adequately, I would have to write another book. But my point here is that communion is meant to bring us to the foot of the cross in gratitude and submission. That's why I prefer to observe it every week. Your church may choose not to, and that's fine; however, I recommend that in every worship service, every week, whether by the direction of your worship team or by your own guidance and motivation, you find a way to proclaim the gospel of the redemption of the Lord Jesus Christ, which he accomplished on the cross and in his resurrection.

Communion is a remembrance, but it is more than a remembrance. It is part of the means God uses to restore our lives.

There is truly no substitute for gathering together with God's people to respond, repent, celebrate, and submit to God. But just the fact that you're doing it with other people means there are likely to be things in worship that you are uncomfortable with or would prefer to do differently. The answer is not to go away and find a church that is more like the one you want to attend; it's to participate and grow along with the other believers in the community where God has planted you.

Whatever style of worship your church embraces, you can incorporate these four crucial elements in your personal experience of corporate worship. As you do, God will use them to awaken your soul and form you into his image.

Personal Reflection

1. What does "corporate worship" mean to you? What role does it play in your life?

2. Which of the four postures of true worship—respond, repent, celebrate, submit—are a regular part of your corporate worship experience? Which, if any, are sometimes missing?

3. In what ways has your experience with worship shaped your life?

4. What has been your experience with liturgy? How might you benefit from more of a personal emphasis on the postures of worship?

5. How much has your experience of worship incorporated the church calendar? How might paying attention to the calendar benefit your walk with Christ?

6. How might your personal preparation for worship enhance the value of the corporate worship experience at your church?

Next Steps

1. Choose one of the four postures of worship—respond, repent, celebrate, submit—that you need to bring to your corporate worship experience this week. Pray that God will help you to worship in this way during this weekend's service.

2. Christian worship always involves storytelling, but sometimes we use shorthand. For example, the word *redemption* has an entire storyline behind it. This weekend in worship, take note of some of the shorthand storytelling that takes place.

3. Consider finding a Bible reading plan that follows the church lectionary, such as the *Book of Common Prayer* or *Book of Common Worship*.

4. Choose at least one additional aspect of the Christian calendar, such as Advent or Lent, to incorporate in your worship experience this coming year.

Chapter 11

COMMUNITY

No matter how much one may love the world as a whole, one can live fully in it only by living responsibly in some small part of it. Where we live and who we live there with define our relationship to the world and to humanity.

—Wendell Berry

oneliness."

That's how a young minister with whom I recently met described the way in which her generation's women feel most broken. She was talking about young adult women, especially those who are married with children. The striking thing for me is that she was also describing women who are actively involved in the local church. But this overwhelming sense of loneliness is hardly limited to that demographic; it spans every age, gender, and social class. As the world's population grows exponentially, loneliness ironically has become a modern psychological epidemic.

It used to be that people would find their sense of connection and belonging within a local community tied to a place. It's hard to describe to those who have never lived in a true community what the community experience is like. And it's hard for those who have never experienced it to imagine their way into it given the opportunity.

Having a community means having a home, a place where you belong. It means knowing and being known, loving and being loved. It means depending on people and having people depend on you. It means giving and receiving grace and forgiveness.

When local communities were the thing, it was most natural for the church to plant itself and grow from within the local community. There was no need for the church to talk of creating community—it already existed. Instead, the church prayed for the transformation of the community so that it reflected the glory of God.

Local communities seem to be a thing of the past now, if by communities we mean neighborhoods where we know and depend on one another. We are a society of commuters; most of us no longer expect to work, shop, eat, socialize, or send our kids to school near the place where we live. The local community is no longer a priority. Now we seem to prefer "regional communities" or even "the global community." As Wendell Berry said, "Many people now feel more at home, and more at ease socially, at a professional convention than in the streets of their own neighborhood."*

Unfortunately, the church, as in other areas, is mimicking rather than truly engaging culture. We've built regional churches that feel more like convention centers than neighborhood gathering places. We seek to attract people from other communities rather than reach our own neighborhoods. The church has little meaningful connection to

---

*Wendell Berry, *The Art of the Commonplace*, ed. Norman Wirzba (Berkeley: Counterpoint Press, 2002), 61.

a place. It is simply one more venue, a destination, like the theater or department store, where people see one another once a week at most and then retreat beyond whatever personal walls of privacy they've erected.

I don't want to disparage the good that has been done by the large, regional churches, but I do believe there have been unintended consequences. One of them has been the further loss of any sense of community—and the loneliness that has become epidemic even within the church.

Our society lost something significant when it lost its local communities. And the church, for the most part, has been a willing accomplice. Ironically, it is also the church that remains in the best position to do something about reversing the trend. And the great thing is that it can all start in a small, local pocket of the kingdom.

Three Metaphors for Christian Community

Christianity is not an individual sport. You cannot follow Jesus in isolation or with people whom you see only once a week for an hour. The church is designed to be a community of faith—a place where, and the means by which, God re-creates his people so that they grow in faith, hope, love, and the fruit of the Spirit.

The true church is a gathering of believers who agree together to help one another grow into the image of our King, Jesus Christ. Some congregations that claim the name "church"—though by no means all—become this kind of assembly. They understand that their reason for existence is to help disciples learn to love God and one another, and they become a training ground for this to happen.

The Greek word for this kind of assembly is *ekklesia*. In the New Testament, it is usually translated "church." The word itself was not originally a spiritual or religious term. It simply meant "assembly" or "gathering." In time, *ekklesia* came to mean much more, but it has never meant less than that.

The author of Hebrews urged his readers to "stir up one another to love and good works, not neglecting to meet together" (Heb. 10:24–25). There is tremendous value in meeting regularly with other Christians, value that goes beyond what you may feel you "get out of it." So the origin of the concept of "church" is found in the need and desire for Christians to gather together in community at particular times and places.

Family

The early church seems to have quickly taken on the form and function of an extended family. Since it was not yet an organized religion, it would not have been possible for local congregations to purchase property or build a worship center. And it didn't take long for them to wear out their welcome in the synagogues. So they began to hold their gatherings for worship and instruction in the homes of believers. As a result, the church naturally organized itself into "households," and this is reflected in some New Testament letters, such as Paul's letter to the Romans (especially chapter 16).

It was a small step then for these small to mid-sized congregations to begin thinking of one another as extended family. They shared resources and looked out for one another's needs. They related to one another with intimacy and affection. The older men and women treated the younger ones as sons and daughters. The young men thought of the young women as sisters, and the women treated the men as brothers. Christians greeted one another with a kiss, just as they would have a family member. When one wept, they all wept, and when one rejoiced, they all rejoiced.

They did life *together*.

To enter the *ekklesia*—the gathering, the church—meant to be adopted by God into his family, with all of the benefits and relationships that entailed.

Body

Another common way that people began to describe the form and function of the *ekklesia* was as a body—the body of Christ. Jesus returned to heaven, but his presence and influence continued to be felt on earth through his body, the church. Christ is the head, and we are his hands and feet, or perhaps some less obvious part of the body that is just as important.

This image of the body emphasizes the *ekklesia*'s unity. The church is not many bodies but one, and there is but one head, Jesus Christ. Christians are most closely connected with their local *ekklesia*; but these local gatherings, no matter their size, are only one expression of the body of Christ. The body of Christ transcends all denominational lines and party affiliations; it transcends all time and space. All who place their faith and hope in Jesus Christ are part of one body. We cannot, therefore, minimize or ignore those with whom we are less comfortable or of whom we lack knowledge.

The body metaphor for the *ekklesia* also emphasizes the diversity of the church. We are not called to be a uniform, monochrome body. Or as the apostle Paul might say, we are not all eyes or ears, tongues or toes. The body of Christ consists of many interdependent members, and this diversity should not be despised or suppressed but appreciated and celebrated. Each part of the body has its unique purpose, and even though we might not yet grasp that purpose, we are not at liberty to disregard any of the body's parts. Certain core beliefs, values, and practices make us who we are as the body of Christ, but beyond that core, there is tremendous room (and need) for diversity.

Pocket of the Kingdom

Finally, it is important to understand how *ekklesia* connects with the kingdom of God. The church is not the kingdom, but it is the temporal, visible expression of the kingdom. Our gatherings of believers function as little pockets of the kingdom wherever and whenever they embrace its beliefs, values, and mission. The church is always an imperfect, limited expression of God's kingdom, but it can nevertheless be a true expression. The more a local church aligns itself with the heart of God, the more it becomes a genuine expression of his kingdom where people can gather and experience a taste of what life will be like when Jesus returns.

Four Functions of True Community

While he doesn't use the word *community* in 2 Corinthians 3:18, I believe Paul was describing its reality when he wrote, "We all, with unveiled face, beholding the glory of the Lord, are being transformed into the same image from one degree of glory to another. For this comes from the Lord who is the Spirit."

Paul had been reminding his Corinthian readers about Moses, who after meeting with God was forced to put a veil over his face because the people could not stand to look at God's glory reflected in his face. Christians, Paul said, should have more confidence. We should be bolder because of the hope that we have in Christ. When we meet together, it should be "with unveiled face." In other words, we should be authentic with one another, not hiding our true identity behind a veil or a mask.

Most of us hide our true selves, not because we're afraid others will be blinded by God's glory but because we want to hide our brokenness. But when Christians come together, Paul said, we should be bold and confident to take off our veils and let other people see us as we are.

When we remove our masks—when we are real with one another—we see God's glory in one another. We think our masks hide our brokenness. In reality, they hide the glory of God in us. When we unveil our faces by being authentic with each other, we see God's handiwork in others and allow others to see it in us. Paul went on to say that when we do this, we are being gradually transformed into God's image.

Here are two reasons, then, why God has given us the *ekklesia*, the church: (1) to give us the opportunity to see his glory, and (2) to give us a means of transformation into his image. This is one reason why the word *church* can be so misleading today: too many people think of church as a place where they go to participate in—or worse, to simply watch—a one-hour service each Sunday.

The assembly of believers was always intended to be so much more.

Telling Stories

Ekklesia provides a great opportunity for Christians to tell one another the true stories about God's redemption. This includes regularly telling the biblical stories of great women and men of faith, such as Deborah, Hannah, Samuel, and Daniel. These stories offer real-life details on what a life of authentic holiness actually looks like. We tell these stories for the same reasons we tell the stories of our biological families: because they help define who we are and, often, what we hope to become.

When we share the stories of our biological families, we don't look for bullet points or principles. These stories operate on a deeper level to shape our identity. So it should be in the body of Christ. We should not be too quick to reduce the biblical stories to mere teaching points or life lessons. Rather, we should tell them because, in some way beyond our understanding, they sculpt our personal story and identity.

Telling the biblical stories will naturally provide a framework for understanding and telling the stories of redemption in our own lives and *ekklesia*. We need to frequently share stories about what God is doing in our lives, church, and community. These stories strengthen our faith, inform our hope, and inspire us to love.

Storing Wisdom

As we regularly share stories, both biblical and personal, the *ekklesia* will naturally become a storehouse of godly wisdom. While wisdom is in one sense a gift, it is also something that we earn by our faith and experience. Wisdom is more than knowing what to believe; it is the capacity to make decisions that honor God and reflect his glory.

Wisdom often comes to us as the result of making poor decisions. If we learn our lessons, we can make better decisions in the future. This is why sharing faith stories is one of the foundations of godly wisdom. Such stories allow us to learn not only from our own experiences but also from the experiences of others within our faith community.

Over time, the community becomes a repository of the "best practices" of faith and life within itself. This kind of corporate wisdom can only come by sharing life together within the *ekklesia*.

While wisdom can at times be captured in pithy sayings and proverbs, we must be careful not to reduce our pursuit of wisdom to a list of sayings. True wisdom requires more than memorizing proverbs and applying them to our lives. It is not a body of knowledge but an intellectual and spiritual capacity that increasingly enables a person to instinctively make the right decision in a given situation.

This sense of discernment cannot be learned in books; it only comes from practical experience in attempting to live a holy life and in sharing life with others who seek to do the same.

Bearing Burdens

As the *ekklesia* shares stories and gleans wisdom in community together, it will almost naturally become a place where Christians help and support one another. As we share stories of what God is doing in our lives, and what we hope he will do, we will at times become aware of another person's need that God has equipped us to help meet. This burden may be physical, social, financial, psychological, or spiritual. While God does not expect us to always fix things or solve one another's problems, he does command us to come alongside and bear one another's burdens (Gal. 6:2).

I said that this happens *almost* naturally. It is natural that we will become aware of one another's needs and burdens as we relate with one another in community. It is even natural to feel pity or compassion for one another. What might be less than natural is to put aside our own needs or priorities in order to reach out to the other person and help carry his load for a time. This requires a conscious decision to roll up our sleeves and get involved, even though it can get messy at times to take an interest in another person's life.

It also requires discernment to recognize needs that are beyond our personal capacity to meet, such as a person who requires professional mental health care. Yet even when someone needs a different kind of help than we can provide, we can still help bear her burdens by connecting her with resources that can help and then staying in touch with her.

The willingness and even eagerness of Christians to bear one another's burdens has historically been one of the most powerful testimonies of the truth of the gospel to the world. Conversely, when professing Christians have failed to love to one another in this way, the witness of the church has suffered great damage.

Participating in a burden-bearing Christian faith community is one of the significant ways that God instills his character in us.

Sharing Responsibility

One final way that *ekklesia* re-creates us in the image of Christ (though others could surely be listed) is by giving us a shared responsibility. I will say much more about mission in the next chapter, but here I want to make the point that Christian mission was never intended to be an individual mandate. God gave the church a mission, and he gave us one another as partners in the endeavor. While every Christian has a role in carrying out the mission of God's kingdom, no Christian anywhere ever bears the weight of the entire mission on his or her shoulders.

We need each other in order to accomplish the task God has given us to do for his kingdom. Our need for one another forces us to take our eyes off ourselves and consider how we can involve others and encourage them in their faith and ministry. It challenges us to learn to relate well with one another and to work with people we might not normally choose to work with. It teaches us that everyone in the community is valuable and has gifts that can contribute to the mission of the kingdom.

As the *ekklesia*, the church, shares life together in community—telling stories of God's redemption, storing the wisdom we gain, bearing one another's burdens, and sharing the responsibility of mission—we reflect God's glory and become more and more like the persons and church God created us to be.

Three Key Attitudes of Christian Community

Many Christians in America today think of the church in the same way that they think of a service provider. They shop around for one that fits their personality and offers what they want for themselves and their family. When they become dissatisfied or simply grow tired of the church they're attending, they look for a new one.

I have always liked Eugene Peterson's words: "You're better off sticking with . . . the 'smallest and nearest church.'"* While I admit that advice is a bit extreme and may not always be the best, I greatly appreciate the principle behind it.

If you shop until you find a church where you feel comfortable and that is made up of people you like, you will miss out on one of the most important ways that *ekklesia* can renew your life. You'll miss out on learning to do life and community with people who are different from you and who will challenge you to grow spiritually in unexpected ways. And you'll miss the opportunity to reflect God's glory to others in the ways God's glory has been reflected by others to you.

Certainly it is helpful to land in a faith community that has a view of faith, discipleship, and mission similar to your own. You also want to avoid a congregation that feels abusive. Other than those concerns, it's usually best to stay put and work through any frustrations, disagreements, or conflicts.

Seek Unity

In what is known as his High Priestly prayer (John 17), Jesus prayed that the church would be united. As you study the letters of Paul, you'll see that he took Jesus' prayer to heart, especially when he found himself at the center of one of the greatest threats to the unity of the young church.

After his conversion, Paul was called by God to extend the invitation to God's kingdom across a significant cultural boundary. With the Jerusalem church's blessing, Paul began preaching the gospel to the Gentiles while Peter and the other disciples focused primarily on the Jews. This led to a major disagreement over how to incorporate

---

*Eugene Peterson, *The Wisdom of Each Other* (Grand Rapids: Zondervan, 1998), 55.

Gentile believers into the *ekklesia*. Some Jewish "conservatives" known as Judaizers thought that Gentile believers in Jesus needed to be circumcised and follow certain aspects of the Jewish Law.

Paul fought against the Judaizers, and after hearing the arguments, the council of Jerusalem mostly sided with him. They agreed that Gentiles did not have to be circumcised and become Jews (Acts 15). However, sometime afterward, it came to Paul's attention that Peter and Barnabas, under the influence of the Judaizers, had stopped having table fellowship with Gentile Christians. Paul knew that this inconsistent treatment had the potential to tear the early church in two, and he vigorously and publicly opposed Peter's capitulation to the Judaizers (Gal. 2).

Paul's letters reflect a passion for the unity of the *ekklesia*, arguing for example that there should be no dividing walls between Jew and Greek, slave and free, male and female (Gal. 3:28). Living in community means recognizing that we have one Lord, one faith, and one hope, and that we should do everything we can to avoid dividing into warring factions.

Practice the Fruit of the Spirit

Living in peace and unity within the church can be difficult. Some might even say it is impossible. But if God commanded it, he will provide the means for us to fulfill his commandment. The major emphasis of this book has been the development of the three Christian virtues—faith, hope, and love—and these three virtues lay the groundwork for our participation in community. The apostle Paul and others also talked about some additional qualities or characteristics that the Holy Spirit produces in the life of Christian believers. They are the fruit of the Spirit: love, joy, peace, patience, kindness, goodness, faithfulness, gentleness, and self-control.

Similarly, the apostle Peter wrote, "Make every effort to supplement your faith with virtue, and virtue with knowledge, and knowledge with self-control, and self-control with steadfastness, and steadfastness with godliness, and godliness with brotherly affection, and brotherly affection with love. For if these qualities are yours and are increasing, they keep you from being ineffective or unfruitful in the knowledge of our Lord Jesus Christ" (2 Peter 1:5–8). It should be easy to see how the fruit of the Spirit would assist our coming together in peace and unity within the community.

Looking at the two passages together, we can see that these qualities are both the fruit of the Spirit and the result of our personal effort, just as with the virtues of faith, hope, and love.

Practice Submission

Perhaps some of the hardest instructions to follow in all of Scripture are those regarding submission. Unfortunately, the church has largely focused on the submission to be exercised between wife and husband. It is important to understand that Paul's instruction for the wife to submit to the husband is a subset of a more comprehensive instruction for all Christians to submit to one another and to those in authority (Eph. 5:21; Rom. 13:1).

The ability to submit to another person does not arise out of low self-esteem or even a proper respect for authority. Rather, it comes from a sense of genuine humility and a desire to consider others as better than ourselves. Submission means putting another's needs ahead of our own. It means placing the community above the individual. It means considering all input and every legitimately held opinion. It means agreeing to disagree and trusting that God will work everything out in the end. It means committing to one another and never holding out the threat to leave if you don't get your way.

Much of the division in the Christian family and the church today can be traced back to a lack of the practice of mutual submission.

Toward Generosity of Spirit

Some of the best experiences I've had of Christian community have been among people who displayed a generosity of spirit towards one another. Some of the worst have been when such a generosity of spirit was lacking in myself or others.

In wrapping up this chapter, I want to share four practical ways Christians can build generosity of spirit into everything they do together as a community.

Make Room

We naturally gravitate toward people who are like us. To have generosity of spirit is to make room for all kinds of people without demanding that they become like us. This means valuing and respecting people of diverse backgrounds and perspectives and making each one feel welcome.

Think the Best

To have generosity of spirit is to assume that people mostly have good intentions even when their words or actions seem wrong to us. The tendency to demonize destroys people and relationships. Thinking the best of others even when they seem wrong to us is the way to strengthen relationships and build toward the future.

Give the Benefit of the Doubt

The best of people will occasionally say or do things that hurt or offend us. Rather than swiftly taking offense, let's instead be ready to give others the benefit of the doubt. There could be any number of explanations for a person's seemingly bad behavior. We should avoid jumping to the worst possible conclusion. We may never know the reasons, and we don't need to. We can simply give the other person the benefit of the doubt—or as Someone else once said, turn the other cheek.

Be Quick to Listen, Slow to Speak

Generosity of spirit takes an interest in the other person, and we show our interest best not when we speak but when we listen.

I will not pretend that living in community is easy. Many have never experienced it and have a hard time imagining what it means and what it looks like. There will be many starts and stops. There will be unexpected challenges and heartbreaks. But given time and intentional effort, God will begin to grow the reality of community within your fellowship of believers. And within that community—that pocket of the kingdom—you will learn to live well and reflect God's glory.

Personal Reflection

1. When have you experienced genuine community in your life?
2. How would you describe what it means to live in community?
3. Which of the four functions of community make community most attractive to you?
4. What aspects of living in community might frustrate or even frighten you?
5. Which of the four aspects of generosity of spirit are most difficult for you? Why?
6. In what specific ways do you think living in genuine community could help you grow in your walk with Christ?

Next Steps

1. Do a community inventory of your life. In what ways are you already experiencing community, even if imperfectly? In what ways would you like to have a greater sense of community?

2. If you are not currently participating in community, think carefully about ways that you could do so, whether by joining an existing group or initiating a new group.

3. If you are already participating in Christian community, exercise your imagination to determine ways in which your community could become a more effective pocket of God's kingdom. Begin talking with others in your group about ways to strengthen it.

4. One of the most powerful witnesses occurs when you can invite a person to experience a fully functioning community of faith. Who do you know who might find such a community attractive? Begin thinking about how you might connect this person to your group or another such group.

Chapter 12

MISSION

Peter says, "Depart from me, because I'm a sinful man," and
Jesus says, "No, actually I've got a job for you."
—N. T. Wright

Travel day today. I'm on the way to the airport at 4 a.m. in a black stretch limousine. So that's a first. (It's a long story and not very interesting.)

My first question when my driver picked me up was, "Are you picking up anyone else?"

"No, unless something changes, we're going directly to the airport."

Good. That means I won't have to make small talk with anyone. I can just sit in the back and write. I hope the driver's not too chatty.

Those, my friends, are the thoughts of an introvert.

They used to make me feel guilty. I used to think I should crave the opportunity to meet new people. That I should be praying for someone to hit with the gospel in those few spare moments. And if I couldn't walk the Romans Road with that person by the time I reached the airport, I would feel guilty. But at least I'd have another shot with someone else on the plane, right?

The airplane conversion story is the ultimate evangelical lore. Every worthy evangelist has a story about helping someone see the light at 40,000 feet. Some people might be gifted that way; I am not.

And that's OK.

The truth is that most people do not begin following Jesus because of a chance encounter. Think about it. How many people who attend your church each weekend were converted after talking with a stranger on an airplane? Where are all of these airplane converts?

I don't doubt such conversions occur, and I've met people who seem to be truly gifted at facilitating them. But I think they are much more the exception than the norm.

I suspect the real reason we place so much hope in this kind of hit-and-run evangelism is because it's self-contained and easy to separate from real life. I can do my duty and know I'll probably never again see the person to whom I've been witnessing. Or it's guilt-induced: "I may be the only chance she has to hear the gospel."

If God gives you an opportunity to witness to someone during a chance encounter, don't let me rob you of the joy of doing so. I've occasionally done the same. (OK, *rarely* is a better word.)

But the people you have the most hope of impacting with the gospel are those who see you live it everyday. And if you talked to them about it constantly, you would more likely drive them crazy than draw them closer to Christ.

Sharing the gospel with others is not about making them our projects. It's about walking with Christ and being open to the opportunity to make a difference in others' lives—sometimes with our words, but not usually *first* with our words.

The mission of the church has always been a corporate mission, not a personal, individual one. Look closely at anyone's story of redemption and you'll likely see that God used not just one person but many people and experiences to guide that individual on the pathway to new life. And many of those who played a part in the journey never did anything so bold as what we might consider "witnessing about Jesus." Often, "a cup of cold water" (Matt. 10:42) offered by a person of faith, though not enough in one sense, is as significant as the actual proclamation of the gospel.

After all, our proclamation of the gospel is also not enough in itself to redeem a person's life; it is simply another tool that God uses to redeem broken people.

So don't overestimate your role in another person's redemption. God will give you a role if you are willing, but its significance will vary depending on the circumstances. And you are never alone; God has already been at work through the Holy Spirit and probably through other Christians to prepare the other person for the gospel message.

It does not all depend on you.

At the same time, neither should you underestimate your role in the Christian mission. While you are but one small part of the church and the Holy Spirit is the one who actively draws men and women to redemption in Christ, the fact is that he involves Christians in the process. He expects that you will be ready to do your part—however big or little—as often as the opportunity arises.

Perhaps nothing makes Christians more fearful than the thought of participating in mission. My desire is for this chapter to demystify the process of Christian mission and give Christians confidence to participate in another person's redemption.

Your role is to be ready to speak the story of redemption—in word and deed—into another person's life. But you are never alone and redemption never depends on you. The mission is a corporate mission;

God gave it to the church around the world and in your community, not to you individually. You participate in Christian mission as a member of the body of Christ—a body part—not as the body itself. And the head of the body is Jesus Christ. He directs the mission, and he writes the story of redemption.

The Essence of Christian Mission

As with most others chapters in this book, whole books have been written about this topic. For the past few years, a debate has raged about the mission of the church. One group says that Christian mission is primarily about proclaiming the gospel; the other insists that it's more about doing good works and promoting social justice.

The question has always mystified me: Why must it be one or the other? Perhaps it is because of the fear and distrust between segments of the church. Some are afraid that if we emphasize good deeds, others will forget the "word" part of the gospel. Others fear that if we emphasize preaching, many will forget the "deed" part of the Gospel.

The answer to the question, I think, is that both are right.

And neither is right.

I hope that clears things up.

Proclaiming the Gospel

Preaching the gospel is absolutely essentially for the success of the Christian mission. Technically, the gospel in the New Testament was the message that "Jesus is Lord." This was a shorthand way of telling the story of redemption in a way that people could quickly make sense of.

In the Greco-Roman world where the Christian message spread most quickly, *gospel* was not a new word. But Paul and others were giving it a new meaning. To the Romans, Caesar was lord. When a new Caesar ascended the throne, or when Caesar's armies conquered a new territory, Roman apostles were sent out to proclaim the gospel—that is, the message of good news—that Caesar was lord. So when Paul travelled throughout the Greco-Roman world proclaiming the gospel that Jesus is Lord, it was an intentionally direct and subversive way of telling the story of Jesus in the language of Caesar's empire. Jesus had been made King, and his apostles were delivering the message that he was offering peace to all who would bow their knee before him and accept his rule over their life.

This was a controversial claim and a powerful message, but we should not forget that it was a translation, so to speak, and not the original language of the message. The original message is found in the Gospels, where Jesus and his disciples proclaimed the arrival of the kingdom of God. In every age, the church is called to proclaim the gospel of God's kingdom in language that speaks to its culture while being faithful to the original message.

It should be clear from the New Testament writings that not every Christian has equal gifting or responsibility for proclaiming the gospel. We are a body; some contribute to the proclamation in one way and some contribute in another. All, however, should be ready to play their part. All should be prepared to share with others the reasons why they have the hope that is within them (1 Peter 3:15). And all should be aware of and seeking opportunities to connect with people who don't yet know Christ.

Doing Good Works

Just as there is no doubt that preaching the gospel is essential for Christian mission, there can be no doubt that doing good works of mercy and social justice are absolutely essential for the success of the Christian mission. Often, Christians look at such activities as extraneous activities—good, but secondary to the Christian mission. This was not Jesus' attitude toward good works. If the Gospels give an accurate representation of Jesus' ministry, it seems he spent as much or more time meeting people's needs than he did proclaiming the gospel in word. For Jesus, good works were not secondary to the gospel or even something that resulted from the gospel. They were part of the gospel. In reality, the gospel message is one that can only be adequately preached in word *and* deed—just as Jesus did in his ministry.

The gospel is about redemption: God re-creating everything that was broken by sin and giving us the opportunity to enjoy eternal life in his kingdom. Jesus' message was that the kingdom of God had arrived, in a provisional way, with his ministry. The fullness of the kingdom is yet to come, but we can experience genuine redemption and a taste of life in God's kingdom today. This means living a life characterized by faith, hope, and love. It is difficult to imagine someone living such a life without being actively involved in doing good works—deeds characterized by mercy and compassion.

Jesus' example shows us that when we meet peoples' genuine needs in his name, we are proclaiming the gospel through our deeds. The question is not whether people can come to Christ through our deeds apart from preaching the Word; it's whether we can genuinely claim the name of Christ if our mission does not include acts of mercy and compassion on behalf of others. The apostle James, for one, argues that we cannot (James 2:14–26). And Paul said that it was what we were created to do (Eph. 2:10).

Making Disciples

I started this section by saying that both those who emphasize gospel proclamation and those who emphasize good works are equally right and wrong. Both are right in the sense that Christian mission cannot be accomplished without either; both are wrong in thinking that Christian mission can be accomplished without the other. To choose one over the other is, in some ways, to do what Paul warned against in 1 Corinthians 12:21. God has given the church members with different gifts and interests, and some can rightfully focus on certain aspects of the mission more than other aspects. None, however, can dismiss the importance of the mission work of other Christians.

In reality, neither proclaiming the gospel nor doing good works is "the mission." The mission is to make disciples (Matt. 28:18–20). Making disciples includes the evangelistic work of proclaiming the gospel, but it is much more than that. It is helping men and women become the people God created them to be ("teaching them to observe all that I have commanded you"), and that certainly includes showing justice and mercy, which Jesus said the Pharisees ought to have done.

In other words, there is no choice to be made between proclaiming the gospel and doing good works. Neither is sufficient alone, and neither can be left undone. Both are essential parts of the church's core mission to make disciples.

Isn't Every Christian to Be a "Soul-Winner"?

Perhaps nothing about the Christian life creates more false guilt than the common expectation that every Christian should be a "soul-winner."

But is this expectation biblical? Does a lack of soul-winning indicate that something is wrong in your Christian life? Does it mean, as some have suggested, that you might not be a Christian at all?

These are serious questions, and they deserve a serious response.

If each disciple is personally responsible for making more disciples, then we certainly need to know that. We never want to make others comfortable in their disobedience and guilt.

On the other hand, it could be that in our genuine zeal to grow the church, to build the kingdom, and—let's face it—to take matters into our own hands, we are placing undue pressure on disciples and creating unnecessary feelings of guilt. We need to know that too.

So let me share a few thoughts, beginning with the Great Commission.

Most of us who grew up in Western civilization have a tendency to read Scripture through a personal, individualistic lens, as if God is speaking through the Bible to me and me alone. So when we come to a text like the Great Commission, our tendency is to apply it to ourselves as individuals, as if it is my personal responsibility to make disciples all by myself.

But the Great Commission is a corporate commission. Those who can read the Greek can confirm that both the imperative ("make disciples") and the participles ("go," "baptizing them," and "teaching them") use the plural construction. In other words, Jesus is addressing the church corporately, not each Christian individually. It's like, "Make disciples together"—or, "All y'all make disciples," for my friends in the American South.

In other words, all of us have a responsibility and a role to play in the Great Commission, but none of us operates independently or on our own. This is consistent with what we see, for example, in Paul's first letter to the Corinthians, where he said that he had planted, Apollos had watered, but God gave the growth (1 Cor. 3:6). As Paul saw it, both he and Apollos had a role to play, but neither were "soul-winners"; that role, apparently, was reserved for God, who provided the increase.

When it comes to evangelism, every Christian has a role to play, but not everyone has the *same* role to play.

Some of us are gifted in offering radical hospitality, not only to friends but also to people we don't yet know or even to those who might be considered our enemies. Others are adept at performing acts of service or mercy for those who are in need.

Some of us do a great job building networks and helping people connect with one another. Others are much better at building relationships with a select few and pouring their lives into that handful.

Some Christians do a great job of teaching and preaching the gospel in large groups. Others are fantastic when it comes to sharing the gospel in one-on-one settings.

And yes, some seem especially gifted at bringing in the harvest, or closing the deal. Interesting, though, that Paul seems reluctant to give the person we consider the "soul-winner" any credit. *God* adds the increase. We're all planters and waterers.

Now, when you put all of these gifts (and more) together into a community of believers, you end up with a powerful witness to the gospel. But put them all out on their own as individuals, operating independently, and their impact will be limited. That's because the Great Commission is a corporate calling.

So to the question, "Is every Christian to be a soul-winner?" the answer is yes, but maybe not in the way you would think. Each of us has a role to play, but none of us does his or her work in isolation. Some of us will be better at planting; others at watering; and some of us, more often than others, will have the privilege of gathering in the harvest.

We should neither overvalue the work of the harvester nor undervalue the work of the planters and waterers.

Whatever role we play, we're all part of God's plan to announce the gospel to the world.

Four Ways Every Christian Can Participate in Mission

Christians often think of mission as a discrete compartment of their lives. When they come to the point in their walk with Christ that they want to reach out to others, they begin to wonder what they can *do* to participate in Christian mission.

Part of the underlying message of this book is that being in mission is not so much about what you do as it is about who you are. People who are growing in faith, hope, and love are becoming the kind of people for whom being in mission is something they do naturally, almost without thinking about it. However, there are some specific things we can do to be sure that we are actively engaging in the Christian mission right where we are.

The following suggestions presume that you are already seeking and growing in the Christian virtues and the fruit of the Spirit. They also assume that you are actively involved in a genuine community of believers where Jesus is recognized as the Lord and Redeemer of your lives, your community, and the world. Such people and communities are naturally attractive to people who are experiencing brokenness in their lives and seeking redemption, even if they don't know where to find it. These suggestions will help to ensure that you're ready for them when they show up in your life.

Practice Hospitality

At their best, Christians have always been and should always be known for their hospitality. In American culture, the word hospitality too often conjures images of Martha Stewart or Rachael Ray busily preparing for guests. The biblical practice of hospitality is at once simpler and more challenging than this cultural image of preparing for the ultimate dinner party. Biblical hospitality is the act of welcoming people, both friends and strangers, into your home for an evening or longer. It is the practical expression of the Messiah's kingdom invitation for any and all to come and be welcomed as family.

Hospitality might include the formal dinner party, but more often it will be a casual gathering with friends or neighbors over dinner or coffee and dessert. There is something about inviting someone into your home that breaks down barriers and paves the way for a deeper relationship. It is an invitation to a deeper level of intimacy. Be intentional about inviting people from your neighborhood, workplace, or community into your home. Get to know them better. As you build relationships, the Holy Spirit will work through them in ways that are beyond your expectation or even your understanding. That's why the practice of biblical hospitality has always been a key part of the church's involvement in mission.

Engage with People in Their Brokenness

As you encounter and build relationships with people in your neighborhood and community, you will undoubtedly meet people who are experiencing some level of suffering in their life. Your first instinct when this happens might be to pull away, to keep your distance. You've heard too many stories of people who take advantage of compassionate people or who don't know how to respect another person's boundaries. You might be afraid that involvement in the life of someone who is broken will become all-consuming. And you don't have time to add something that will be all-consuming to your schedule. But if you never engage with people in their brokenness, you will miss a tremendous opportunity to bring the message of redemption into their lives, whether by word or deed.

Yes, it is advisable to proceed cautiously in helping people who are suffering, especially when you barely know them. And yes, some circumstances are too overwhelming or beyond the expertise of someone not professionally trained to care for hurting people. Yet it is clear from the gospels that Jesus intends for us to engage in the brokenness of others. Part of our response to the Great Commission is to recognize that brokenness and to communicate to the broken in word and deed the message of Christ's redemption. In most cases, this takes time; it requires engaging with people long enough to build a relationship of trust. And this can't be done from a distance. As you have opportunity, draw the hurting person into your community of faith. This is one of the great values of Christian community—that together you can walk alongside the hurting so that the burden doesn't fall entirely on any one person.

Discover and Use Your Gifts

Your greatest contribution to the Christian mission will occur in areas where you have been gifted by the Holy Spirit for ministry. Therefore it is important that you discover what gifts God has given you and then make a conscious effort to use those gifts in your local community.

Be Ready to Give Reason for Your Hope

Most Christians at some time will hear stories of "buttonhole evangelists"—people adept at sharing the gospel with someone they've only just met in a way that elicits an immediate confession of faith in Christ. Without making any judgment about the merits of such an evangelistic approach, I want to reassure you that it is not the norm for Christian witness. Most effective evangelism takes place in the context of existing relationships.

The Bible does not impose on Christians the expectation that we will use a cold-turkey evangelistic approach, nor does it expect that everyone will have the success or even the boldness of the apostle

Paul. Paul apparently was the exception rather than the standard against which we should measure ourselves. At least that makes more sense to me than the alternative—that the rest of us are utter failures.

Instead, what the Bible expects is that when opportunities come your way, you will be ready to give a reason for the hope you have in Christ. This doesn't mean that you should simply sit around and wait for people to ask. As you offer hospitality, engage with people in their brokenness, and live out a life of faith, hope, and love, you will have opportunities to share your hope. Be ready for those and bold when they occur.

In addition to helping you find healing, hope, and holiness, this book is my attempt to help you do just that: be prepared to give a reason for the hope that is within you. The goal is for you to become a disciple who makes disciples—not on your own, but within a pocket of the kingdom. And I've tried to proclaim the gospel to you in such a way that it is easy for you to share it with others. A portable message for a portable temple.

A Portable Temple

In chapter 3, you learned the biblical truth that in Christ, you are God's temple. God's Spirit lives in you. To wrap up this final chapter, let's look at three key ways this truth empowers your mission.

Wherever You Go, God's Spirit Is There Too

The temple in Jerusalem represented God's dwelling place on earth. It was the place where heaven and earth intersected. God's Spirit rested in the inner sanctuary, the Holy of Holies. Now, the temple has gone portable. Wherever two or three are gathered in his name, his Spirit is in the midst.

Even more, your body is the temple of the Holy Spirit. Wherever you go, you carry the Spirit with you. As you go and make disciples, however that looks for you, you never go alone. God's Spirit is with you, strengthening and empowering you for mission.

Wherever You Go, You Reflect God's Glory

The temple in Jerusalem was the place where people would experience God's presence in all of its glory and majesty. Now, instead of an architectural structure, *you*—unbelievable as it sounds—have become a place where, and a means by which, people can encounter God.

People see Jesus in you.

Most of the time you won't be aware that it's happening, and that's for the best, but follow Jesus and you will reflect his glory. Never perfectly, but genuinely. You can count on it.

Wherever You Go, You Are an Agent of God's Redemption

The temple in Jerusalem was the place where God's people looked for and found redemption. Now that you are God's temple, you have become an agent of God's redemption. Not that you can do anything to save or redeem a person's life on your own. Neither could the temple. But God can use you—again, most often when you're not aware of what he's doing through you—to bring redemption to other people's lives.

When the church is gathered, equipped, and sent, we are sent to be portable temples, taking God's glory, presence, and redemption to the world. That is not something you can do by your own power or intention.

What you *can* do is live well, pursuing holiness—putting off the works of the sinful nature and putting on faith, hope, love, and the fruit of the Spirit. As you cooperate with the Holy Spirit to add these virtues and fruit to your life, God will work through you to spread his glory. He will make you his temple.

Personal Reflection

1. What personal attitudes and experiences do you bring to the idea of Christian mission?
2. What about Christian mission makes you feel enthusiasm? Anxiety?
3. How do you think word and deed work together to make disciples?
4. What do you think is each Christian's personal responsibility for Christian mission?
5. Of the four ways every Christian can participate in mission, which do you need to be more involved in?
6. What has been the biggest impact this book has made on your life? How will you pass on its message to others?

Next Steps

1. Pray and ask God to help you come to grips with your personal responsibility for the corporate mission of the church.
2. Spend some time talking with a mature Christian who knows you. Request his or her thoughts on how you can best contribute to Christian mission.
3. Choose one of the four ways every Christian can participate in mission and focus the next forty days on making that a lasting practice of your life.
4. Thank God for the ways he is re-creating you and making a place for you in his plan to redeem the world.

❖ ❖ ❖

But the Helper, the Holy Spirit, whom the Father will send in my name, he will teach you all things and bring to your remembrance all that I have said to you. Peace I leave with you; my peace I give to you. Not as the world gives do I give to you. Let not your hearts be troubled, neither let them be afraid. (John 14:26–27)

Jesus said to them again, "Peace be with you. As the Father has sent me, even so I am sending you." And when he had said this, he breathed on them and said to them, "Receive the Holy Spirit. If you forgive the sins of any, they are forgiven them; if you withhold forgiveness from any, it is withheld." (John 20:21–23)

AFTERWORD

Before breakfast one morning, my daughter and I walked out behind our house to our garden beds.

We were surprised to see several sprouts that weren't there the night before—cucumbers, pumpkins, watermelon, squash, basil, parsley. Several other plants had grown noticeably overnight.

"It's interesting," Courtney said, "how you never see plants growing; you only see that they've grown."

And really, that's the way it is with all living things.

I'm with my children almost every day, but I've never been able to capture the moment when their frame pushed up another inch. I've only been able to see their growth in retrospect.

I remember imagining what my oldest baby girl would look like all grown up. Now, as she approaches age eighteen, she is more beautiful, more like her mother, than even I imagined she would be.

I can't pinpoint when it happened. And I certainly didn't do anything to make it happen.

She has had to endure more storms than I would have preferred, but they've made her stronger. She has seen more grief and brokenness than I would have chosen for her. But as she places her trust in Jesus, he redeems every moment in ways that are beyond my comprehension.

Parenting, like gardening, is an exercise in patience. There's little you can do to make a plant grow other than planting it in good soil, keeping the area clear of predators, and providing the right amount of moisture and nutrients. Try to do more than that and you often end up doing more harm than good.

Remember when you were a child and an adult would tell you how much taller you had grown? Most children feel proud when someone notices they're taller, but it usually takes someone else pointing it out for them to realize that it has happened.

But how silly would it be to set goals for your child's height?

"By next summer, young man, I'd like to see you put on three more inches!"

No, we know that there are limits to how much and how quickly our children can grow.

Yet when it comes to our own growth in Christ, we have different expectations.

We want to see ourselves grow today.

We want to know how we can be fully grown by tomorrow.

We want instant maturity.

We want the strength without the storms.

We want the depth without the brokenness.

We want to follow Christ spontaneously without submitting to his discipline.

We want to *feel* ourselves grow. Right now!

But if we would stop and reflect for just a moment, we would know it doesn't work that way.

Growth takes time.

And patience.

You can't see yourself grow; you can only see that you've grown. And probably only when others point it out to you.

To grow in your walk with Christ, make sure you're planted in the right kind of soil. Be with people who contribute to your growth. Watch out for predators.

And don't expect to see yourself growing—but believe it when someone says you are.

Measure your growth not in days or weeks but in years and decades. And give God the glory that you are not the same person you were three or five years ago.

Imagine the person you can become when God fully matures you.

Nurture his life in you and wait patiently for the Redeemer of all things to do his work in you too.

RECREATABLE
SMALL GROUP
DISCUSSION GUIDE

Chapter One: Shards

Engage

1. Have you ever had someone who knew what he was doing fix something you thought was broken beyond repair? Share your story with the group.
2. Do you think most people find it easy to connect with their brokenness? Why or why not?

Examine

3. How do you think the three attitudes—discontent, distrust, and disregard—lead to broken relationships?
4. How does sin affect the four relationships—with self, others, God, and creation? Explain your answer.
5. Do you agree that it's important for Christians to embrace not only their sinfulness but also their brokenness? Give reasons for your answer.

Equip

6. In what ways have you seen discontent, distrust, or disregard lead to brokenness in your life or in others' lives?

7. Do you think it's possible for Jesus to pick up the broken pieces of our lives and relationships and put them together again? What might that look like?

8. Do you think it's possible for people to learn to conduct their lives so that they bring healing and redemption to the world rather than introducing more brokenness? What might that look like?

Empower

9. How can we as a group help one another to recognize the ways in which our attitudes and actions introduce brokenness into the world?

10. How can we as a group help one another begin to find redemption and healing in Jesus Christ?

Chapter Two: Glory

Engage

1. Have you ever had a time in your life or been to a place where you thought, "This is what life was meant to be"? Describe that time and place for the group.

2. Describe for the group what you imagine life would be like in a world where there was no sin or brokenness.

Examine

3. As you understand it, based on this chapter, what was the first man and woman's original calling?

4. Based on this chapter, what was God's plan for putting back together again what Adam and Eve broke in the garden? Describe the plan with as much detail as possible.

5. What do you think it means when we say that Jesus is Lord? What do you think it means when we say Jesus is Redeemer?

Equip

6. How do you understand your calling in life? How does it connect with our common calling to reflect God's glory?

7. What are some of the ways a person's brokenness could cause that person to fall short of the calling God has given him or her?

8. What role do you think pockets of the kingdom play in helping people to live out God's calling on their lives?

Empower

9. What practical difference do you think it would make if our group were to see itself not just as a study group but as a pocket of Christ's kingdom?

10. What role do you think we can play to help one another learn to reflect God's glory in our lives and relationships?

Chapter Three: Intersection

Engage

1. Describe for the group a place where you seem to connect easily with God. What is it about the place that makes it such a special point of contact?

2. Share with the group a particular person in whom you find it easy to see Christ. What about the person makes Christ so visible to you?

Examine

3. Do you think some places are more sacred than others? If so, how do such places become sanctified?
4. What would you say was the importance of the tabernacle and temple for God's people?
5. How would you describe the new "intersection" that was created when Jesus died and rose again?

Equip

6. What difference does it make to be aware that God dwells in other Christians?
7. Do you think a person should consciously try to "be Christ" for someone else? Why or why not?
8. What might it look like for a group of believers to sanctify a place (outside the church building) to help others connect with God?

Empower

9. What do you think it would look like for our group to be a "temple" in our neighborhood or community?
10. How can we as a group encourage one another to see that God's Spirit lives in each of us individually wherever we go?

Chapter Four: Holy

Engage

1. Has your experience with Christianity, both personally and in the church, leaned more toward pessimism or optimism regarding holiness? What impact do you think this has had on your life?
2. Why do people tend to think of holiness as scary or otherwise intimidating?

Examine

3. What do you think of the statement that holiness is more about always intending to get things right than about never doing anything wrong? Do you agree or disagree? Why?

4. From a biblical perspective, how would you describe or define a fully mature human being? What elements or characteristics are important to include?

5. What was the difference between clean, unclean, and holy in the Jewish culture? How does this help you understand the biblical demand for holiness in your life?

Equip

6. What do you think it would take to help you or another Christian develop a more optimistic perspective toward holiness?

7. What are some of the obstacles Christians face in discovering the gifts God has given them? What are some of the things that have helped you in this area?

8. Share with the group a time when you felt utterly defeated in your walk with Christ. What helped you to get through that time? Or what do you need right now to help you walk in a manner worthy of your calling?

Empower

9. How can we as a group help one another develop a culture of optimism regarding holiness?

10. How can we as a group most effectively help each other identify our unique gifts and take on appropriate responsibility in the kingdom?

Chapter Five: Sustainable

Engage

1. Have you ever felt like you weren't good enough, couldn't do enough, or would never measure up to the typical expectations of the Christian life? What is or was that like for you?

2. Consider that following Jesus could become as natural for you as walking. Do you find that idea attractive? Do you think it's realistic? Why or why not?

Examine

3. How much confidence do you think a Christian should have about his or her ability to learn to walk with Christ?

4. In what ways is growing in Christ like developing physical muscle memory? In what ways is it different?

5. How do you think a person's mind, will, and heart work together to determine how a person acts?

Equip

6. How do you think a Christian can go about developing virtues in his or her life?

7. What obstacles might a Christian need to overcome in order to develop spiritual muscle memory?

8. What are specific ways a Christian can learn to manage his or her thoughts and emotions?

Empower

9. In what ways do you think our community of believers can help one another develop spiritual muscle memory?

10. How can our group encourage and challenge one another without inadvertently placing unrealistic expectations on each other?

Chapter Six: Faith

Engage

1. When was the last time you experienced a crisis of faith? Can you describe the experience? Do you think the crisis began with your mind, heart, or will? Explain.

2. How would you personally describe the core content of the Christian faith?

Examine

3. How does this chapter present the three components of faith? What examples would you give of the different kinds of faith?

4. What do you think of the "Six Essential Truths" described in this chapter? Do you believe that all six truths really are essential? Were any essential truths left out?

5. Which of the truths would you most like to learn more about? What specific questions or concerns do they raise for you?

Equip

6. Do you think of faith struggles more as crises or as opportunities? Why?

7. How do you think a Christian can turn a faith crisis into an opportunity for growth?

8. What are some strategies you personally could use to cultivate your belief in the gospel, your trust in it, or your loyalty to it?

Empower

9. If we were to create a list of five to seven essential truths of the gospel according to our group, what would those truths be and how would we state each one?

10. This chapter suggests that doctrine is important mostly because it gives us a quick summary of the story of redemption. How can we as a group affirm the importance of doctrine while continuing to emphasize and be shaped by the story?

Chapter Seven: Hope

Engage

1. Why do you think hope so often gets less attention than faith and love in Christian life and teaching?
2. What are some reasons why you see hope as an important virtue in the Christian life? What would be the ramifications of having no hope?

Examine

3. What is the difference between knowing God's plans for the future and anticipating them?
4. Which aspect of the Christian hope after Christ returns—resurrection, new creation, judgment, and glory—appeals to you most, and why? Which is most challenging for you?
5. What aspect of the Christian hope here and now—a new creation, restored relationships, pockets of the kingdom, and the Holy Spirit—appeals to you most, and why? Which is most challenging for you?

Equip

6. What difference do you think it could make in a Christian's life to actively anticipate the future God has planned for him or her?
7. What would it mean to live each day in the power of the resurrection? What makes this difficult? What helps you to do it?

8. What do you think prevents some churches or small groups from becoming the pockets of the kingdom described in this chapter?

Empower

9. What are some things that make it difficult to be a person of hope? In what ways can we help one another be persons of hope?
10. What changes can we make in our group to become a more effective pocket of the kingdom?

Chapter Eight: Love

Engage

1. What makes it difficult to maintain an attitude of worship throughout the week?
2. What are some of the reasons people might find it difficult to genuinely love their neighbors?

Examine

3. What do you think Jesus meant when he said that the way to inherit eternal life is to love God and your neighbor?
4. Do you agree that when you act in love, the feelings will follow? Why or why not? What examples can you share?
5. How do you think worship and submission (obedience) help us grow in our love for God? How do respect and submission (service) help us grow in our love for others?

Equip

6. What are some key ways you can express love for God with your thoughts? Your emotions? Your actions?

7. What are some key ways you can express love for your neighbors with your thoughts? Your emotions? Your actions?

8. How have you seen God redeem relationships in your life or in the lives of those you love? What were some of the key ways that redemption occurred?

Empower

9. What role do you think a group like ours can play in helping one another learn to love God?

10. How would you like our group to help you learn to love others and find redemption in your relationships?

Chapter Nine: Scripture

Engage

1. What challenges or frustrations have you experienced with reading the Bible?

2. What do you think about the idea that your Bible reading plan needs to fit your personality and reading style?

Examine

3. What difference do you think it makes that the Bible was written for a community?

4. How do you think the Bible can help Christians connect with their heritage and culture?

5. Why is it significant that the Bible is essentially an unfinished narrative?

Equip

6. What has really helped you connect with Scripture?

7. How has seeing the Bible as a story helped you in your walk with Christ? What role has doctrine played?

8. In what ways do you think the Bible should shape the culture of a Christian community?

Empower

9. What do you imagine are the best ways for our group to read Scripture so that it shapes our life together?
10. What role do you think this group can play in helping one another keep the larger story of Scripture in mind?

Chapter Ten: Worship

Engage

1. Why do you think worship tends to be such a controversial topic in the church?
2. Have you ever had an experience of heaven intersecting earth in worship? How would you describe it?

Examine

3. What do you think of the four postures of worship that were described? Are there any additional attitudes you would add?
4. What about the four ways to participate in worship? Are there other key behaviors you would add?
5. What do you believe is meant by the statement that worship, over time, helps us become more like God as well as more human? Do you agree? How might it work?

Equip

6. In what circumstances might it be appropriate for a Christian to try to influence the way his church does worship? When might it not be appropriate to do so?

7. Do you think it's possible for a Christian to bring additional elements to her private experience of corporate worship? In what ways have you done this?

8. Are there any elements of worship described in this chapter that you would like to incorporate more into your worship experience? What are they and why?

Empower

9. Are there ways that we as a group can broaden or enrich the practice of corporate worship in each others' lives? What might they be?

10. How do you think we can find unity in the midst of diverse preferences about the worship experience?

Chapter Eleven: Community

Engage

1. Do you agree that loneliness is epidemic in modern society? What evidence would you point to?

2. If genuine community is so attractive to people, why do so many find it hard to participate in?

Examine

3. What can we learn from the metaphor of the church as a family?

4. What can we learn from the metaphor of the church as the body of Christ?

5. What can we learn from the metaphor of the church as a pocket of Christ's kingdom?

Equip

6. Of the four functions of true community, which do you think the church generally does a pretty good job with?

7. Of the four functions of true community, which does the church generally need to do more effectively?

8. How can the church help people envision true community and learn to participate in it?

Empower

9. What obstacles to participating in community do you see? How might people overcome such obstacles?

10. What outside forces sometimes prevent people from being in community? How might people counteract those forces?

Chapter Twelve: Mission

Engage

1. What has helped you most in our study of this book, *ReCreatable*?

2. What anxieties or bad experiences do you bring with you to your thinking about Christian mission?

Examine

3. From a biblical point of view, what do you think is the relationship between proclaiming the gospel and doing good works?

4. What do you believe is a Christian's responsibility regarding the Great Commission?

5. Do you agree that a Christian's unique role and responsibility in mission is likely consistent with his or her gifts and personal identity? Why or why not?

Equip

6. What do you think are ways we can reduce some of the guilt and anxiety people feel about mission while still challenging people to participate in it?

7. How can a church or Christian community not only proclaim the gospel and do good works but also make disciples who are making disciples?

8. What are some ways that you plan to participate in Christian mission in the future? How can our group help and support you?

Empower

9. In what ways do you think our study has empowered you to be a disciple who makes disciples—not on your own but working together with other believers?

10. What has been the biggest impact this book has made on your life? How will you share its message with others?